Sharing Books for Social and Emotional Understanding

MARGARET GOLDTHORPE AND PERDY BUCHANAN-BARROW

PERMISSION TO PHOTOCOPY

This book contains materials which may be reproduced by photocopier or other means for use by the purchaser. The permission is granted on the understanding that these copies will be used within the educational establishment of the purchaser. The book and all its contents remain copyright. Copies may be made without reference to the publisher or the licensing scheme for the making of photocopies operated by the Publishers' Licensing Agency.

The rights of Margaret Goldthorpe and Perdy Buchanan-Barrow to be identified as the authors of this work have been asserted by them in accordance with sections 77 and 78 of the Copyright, Designs and Patents Act 1988.

Sharing Books for Social and Emotional Understanding
MT10009
ISBN-13: 978 1 85503 407 5
ISBN-10: 1 85503 407 7
© Margaret Goldthorpe and Perdy Buchanan-Barrow
Illustrations © Mike Phillips and Rebecca Barnes

All rights reserved
First published 2006
Reprinted 2006

Printed in the UK for LDA
Abbeygate House, East Road, Cambridge, CB1 1DB, UK

ACKNOWLEDGEMENTS

As ever, there are many people to thank. We want to thank all the staff and pupils of Alexandra School, in particular Suzy and Emily, for trying out so many of the activities. Thank you to Dennis for some inspirational assemblies and the time and space to do this work. We would also like to thank our families, who have put up with no food and messy houses and served us tea on an hourly basis. And finally a big thank you to Corin, our helpful and encouraging editor.

ACKNOWLEDGEMENTS

7   INTRODUCTION

8   USING THIS BOOK IN SCHOOL

10   RUNNING A CLASS DEBATE

12   INDEX BY BOOK AND TOPIC

14   DETAILS OF PICTURE BOOKS FEATURED

15   CLASSROOM AND HOME MATERIALS

BOOK 01   16   ALL JOIN IN

BOOK 02   20   MISTER MAGNOLIA

BOOK 03   24   ALFIE WEATHER

BOOK 04   28   GRANDFATHER'S PENCIL AND THE ROOM OF STORIES

BOOK 05   32   DOWN THE DRAGON'S TONGUE

BOOK 06   36   OWL BABIES

BOOK 07   40   THE BEAR UNDER THE STAIRS

BOOK 08   44   LOVELY OLD ROLY

BOOK 09   48   OSCAR GOT THE BLAME

BOOK 10   52   ON THE WAY HOME

BOOK 11   56   THE TRUE STORY OF THE 3 LITTLE PIGS!

BOOK 12   60   THE PRINCESS KNIGHT

BOOK 13   64   WHERE THE WILD THINGS ARE

BOOK 14   68   SUSAN LAUGHS

BOOK 15   72   LOOK WHAT I'VE GOT!

BOOK 16   76   SOMETHING ELSE

BOOK 17   80   SLOW LORIS

BOOK 18   84   THE SMARTEST GIANT IN TOWN

BOOK 19   88   KATIE MORAG DELIVERS THE MAIL

BOOK 20   92   AMAZING GRACE

BOOK 21   96   DOGGER

101   PHOTOCOPIABLE RESOURCES

111   TRAINING

CONTENTS

Introduction

This is a book about books. Each of the main sections takes a well-known and easily available storybook and provides the teacher with the following guidance for when they share it with their children: story details, relevant discussion points, circle-time ideas and follow-up activities. These are designed to help each child engage fully with the story and with its characters' lives and dilemmas, so that they may, after experiencing the story, have a deeper understanding of themselves, their own lives and their relationships.

As teachers, we often wish we could encourage the parents of the children in our classes to have discussions with their children about social and emotional issues. To this end, each classroom section has corresponding materials for home use. These include story details, discussion points and ideas for relevant practical activities that parents can undertake with their child at home. The materials can be sent home with a copy of the storybook for the children to explore.

It is important to stress that the discussion points and activities for home are not in any way related to academic work. Rather they are designed to encourage discussion between the parent and the child about feelings, attitudes, opinions, beliefs and relationships, with all their attendant joys and problems – to enable both parent and child to grow in their understanding and their relationship.

This book aims to encourage, and enable, parents and children to share and develop their emotional literacy together, enjoying sharing a book, perhaps snuggled up on the sofa.

Virginia Woolf once said that books should have a before and after effect, in that we should not be quite the same people after we have read a book as we were before. We hope that this book contributes to your experience and to that of the children you teach and their families.

INTRODUCTION

Using this book in school

We have found that the best way to approach each storybook is as follows.

PRIOR TO THE LESSON

- **Read the story all the way through to yourself.**

- **Look carefully at the illustrations as they will reveal lots of subtleties that will be of use later.**

- **Read the relevant classroom and home sections.**

- **Photocopy the classroom material and annotate or highlight it until you feel that you have a working document you are comfortable with.**

DURING THE LESSON

- **Read the story straight through to the children.**

- **Re-read the story, bringing up the talking points from the classroom material in the way you choose as you go along.**

Each classroom section contains the following:

- story details; • a summary of the story;

- talking points; • circle-time suggestions, including games and sentence stems to serve as the beginning of rounds;

- ideas for follow-up activities designed to help children explore the themes of the story in greater depth.

Some classroom sections also include the following:

- ideas for assemblies; • motions for class debates.

EXPLORING A THEME WITH THE WHOLE SCHOOL

Assemblies are a wonderful opportunity to explore complex emotional themes with the whole school. You might like to choose one of the stories to share in assembly, through reading, acting it out, or having a presentation showing the work of a class that has already studied the book.

You could follow this up by having the whole school take up the theme. For example, classes could read and discuss the book, hold circle times, hold a formal debate, and display their ideas on noticeboards. The theme could also be a focus for school council discussions.

After a week (or more) of whole-school consideration of the theme, you could have a final assembly to share the work and ideas of the whole school.

Throughout this book you will find that several of the lesson plans include pre-planned assemblies.

CHILDREN EXPERIENCING SOCIAL AND EMOTIONAL DIFFICULTIES

You may choose to use a storybook and the attendant ideas for individual work with a specific child who is experiencing a similar problem. For example, you may have a fairly lively child who might connect with *Where the Wild Things Are*. Alternatively, *Something Else* could chime with a child who seems a rather solitary soul.

USING THE HOME PAGES

We suggest that you photocopy the home section for each story, and also the 'Sharing books at home' page (page 102). These could be stapled to or inserted in the front of the relevant storybook, or kept with the book in a plastic wallet. This would mean that when a book goes home for a child to share with their family, there will be pages outlining some points for discussion and some ideas for relevant activities supplied with the book.

Books can be sent home on a regular basis as part of the home/school reading programme, or in addition to this provision. You could try to get hold of a set of a particular book by contacting your library service in advance or by using resources within the school. You could, over time, buy sets of books for use with these materials so that you build up a collection. You will then be able to send the books home for a range of children over a two- to three-week period during which you may choose to work on one of the storybooks.

The home pages could also be used by teaching assistants working with groups or individuals in the classroom.

PLANNING AND RECORD KEEPING

We have included two planning sheets on pages 103 and 104, one for the classroom and one for home. You can use these to devise work for storybooks that are not covered in this publication.

As it can be hard to show evidence of children's social and emotional learning, it can be useful to keep photocopies and work generated in a ring binder. A digital camera can be useful for taking photographs of large-scale activities, noticeboards and so on. This file could then become a resource and record for the school. This might also be useful evidence for school inspections.

CHILD PROTECTION

In the course of sharing a story or during the follow-up activities, a child may disclose something that you believe to be a child protection issue. You should handle such situations with care, compassion and sensitivity. You need to explain to the child what may happen next, who will be told and what they will do. All your actions need to be in accordance with your school's policy on child protection. It is important not to offer complete confidentiality. LEA guidelines stress that teachers should disclose relevant information regarding the protection of children to the school's child protection co-ordinator.

Running a class debate

In many of the 'For the classroom' sections we suggest running a class debate on a particular issue that arises in the story. We have run a range of debates with children of a wide spectrum of abilities and ages, from both KS1 and KS2. Although it might seem a quite formal approach to take, the debates produced some of the most amazing speaking and listening from children that we had ever seen. With this in mind, we have provided you with some guidelines so that you too can see the impact that this approach can have:

- Give the children warning about the topic to be debated. This can be done in the form of homework. Each child has to think of at least two reasons to support each side of the debate.

- If the topic for debate seems challenging, it might be worth having a short discussion with the whole class before setting the homework, to give them time to formulate some ideas and to establish some guidelines.

- It is useful to have at least two adults in class for the debate. The teacher can chair the debate, while another adult can scribe.

- The job of the scribe is to record on a flipchart the key points made by each side during the debate. At the end of the debate, the chairperson can use these notes to summarise the points made by each side, which may help the audience to vote.

- There will be two groups of children: one group to propose the motion and one group to oppose it. We usually called the group proposing the motion the green team, while the opposing group are called the red team. There can be up to four children in each group.

- Before the debate begins, each group should spend a few minutes, with an adult if possible, discussing their points and the order in which they will raise them. Within a group of four, for example, the first child could mention the key points, the second and third children could expand on them or respond to points made by the other group, and the last child could sum up their group's argument.

- For the first debate, choose two groups who will be able to demonstrate to the rest of the class how it is done. These children will need good speaking and listening skills. In subsequent weeks, each group needs one child who has good speaking and listening skills.

- The rest of the class will be the audience for the debate. Explain that they have a responsibility to listen, ask questions, make comments and vote.

- The debate begins with the proposing group outlining their key points. The opposing group can then reply, outlining their key points.

- The second and third child in the proposing group then develop some of their team's main points and, if appropriate, attempt to counter some of the opposing group's main points. The second and third children in the opposing team reply in the same manner.

- At this stage, you could open the debate to the floor. Participants can ask the groups questions to explore the issue further.

- One way of ensuring that the same two children don't ask all the questions in each debate is to give each child in the audience a coloured brick of some kind. As a child asks a question or makes a comment, they give you their brick. You can keep track of children who always have a brick left at the end of a debate, and encourage them to contribute next time. The very talkative children will have to edit their ideas and select what they most want to say.

- Once you have allowed a series of questions to be asked of each group, allow the final child in each group to summarise their group's position.

- Then the audience have to vote. For the purposes of voting, it is useful to have a set of coloured cards, green on one side and red on the other. These can be made with some white card and coloured sticky-backed plastic, or by sticking two thin pieces of different coloured card together. After the points for each side have been summarised, the audience are asked to vote by holding up their card, showing the colour of the group they support. Adults do not vote as some children are likely to copy them. Children should be encouraged to vote on the strength of the arguments and not be swayed by friendship.

- At the end of the debate, we encourage the two groups to shake hands and congratulate each other on a good debate.

GUIDELINES

	Worries and fears	Living with siblings	Helping others	Friendship and belonging	Making the most of every day	Imaginary friends	Responsibility and blame	Understanding differences	Missing Mum	Doing the right thing	Being honest	Bullying	Using our imagination
All Join In			★	★	★								★
Mister Magnolia				★	★								★
Alfie Weather			★		★								★
Grandfather's Pencil and the Room of Stories													
Down the Dragon's Tongue	★				★								
Owl Babies	★	★							★				
The Bear under the Stairs	★												
Lovely Old Roly													
Oscar Got the Blame						★	★			★			
On the Way Home							★				★		★
The True Story of the 3 Little Pigs!							★				★		
The Princess Knight		★						★					
Where the Wild Things Are				★						★			
Susan Laughs				★	★			★					
Look What I've Got!					★			★					★
Something Else				★				★				★	
Slow Loris				★				★					
The Smartest Giant in Town			★		★					★			
Katie Morag Delivers the Mail							★			★	★		
Amazing Grace	★							★					
Dogger	★	★	★							★			

INDEX BY BOOK AND TOPIC

Inclusion	Being part of a family	Sorting out problems	Making choices	Valuing special things	Transfer to a new school	Forgiveness	Bereavement and loss	Misbehaviour	Valuing memories	Exploring reputation	Jealousy	Being a hero	Asking for help
	★												
	★												
	★		★					★					
	★	★							★				
													★
	★					★		★					
	★						★		★				
									★				
		★							★				
		★										★	
	★	★		★	★		★		★				
★													
			★							★			
★													
				★					★				
		★										★	
	★	★			★								★
		★											
	★	★		★								★	★

13

Details of picture books featured

All Join In
Author and illustrator: Quentin Blake
Publisher: Red Fox Picture Books (1992)
ISBN: 0 09 996470 8

Mister Magnolia
Author and illustrator: Quentin Blake
Publisher: Red Fox Picture Books (1999)
ISBN: 0 09 940042 1

Alfie Weather
Author and illustrator: Shirley Hughes
Publisher: Red Fox Picture Books (2002)
ISBN: 0 09 940425 7

Grandfather's Pencil and the Room of Stories
Author and illustrator: Michael Foreman
Publisher: Red Fox Picture Books (1995)
ISBN: 0 09 950331 X

Down the Dragon's Tongue
Author: Margaret Mahy
Illustrator: Patricia MacCarthy
Publisher: Frances Lincoln Ltd (2001)
ISBN: 0 7112 1617 7

Owl Babies
Author: Martin Waddell
Illustrator: Patrick Benson
Publisher: Walker Books Ltd (1994)
ISBN: 0 7445 3167 5

The Bear under the Stairs
Author and illustrator: Helen Cooper
Publisher: Corgi Children's Books (1994)
ISBN: 0 552 52706 8

Lovely Old Roly
Author: Michael Rosen
Illustrator: Priscilla Lamont
Publisher: Frances Lincoln Ltd (2002)
ISBN: 0 7112 1489 1

Oscar Got the Blame
Author and illustrator: Tony Ross
Publisher: Red Fox Picture Books (1995)
ISBN: 0 09 957280 X

On the Way Home
Author and illustrator: Jill Murphy
Publisher: Macmillan Children's Books (1982)
ISBN: 0 333 37572 6

The True Story of the 3 Little Pigs!
Author: Jon Scieszka
Illustrator: Lane Smith
Publisher: Puffin Books (1991)
ISBN: 0 14 054056 3

The Princess Knight
Author: Cornelia Funke
Illustrator: Kerstin Meyer
Publisher: The Chicken House (2001)
ISBN: 1 904442 14 5

Where the Wild Things Are
Author and illustrator: Maurice Sendak
Publisher: Red Fox Picture Books (2000)
ISBN: 0 09 940839 2

Susan Laughs
Author: Jeanne Willis
Illustrator: Tony Ross
Publisher: Red Fox Picture Books (2001)
ISBN: 0 09 940756 6

Look What I've Got!
Author and illustrator: Anthony Browne
Publisher: Walker Books Ltd (1996)
ISBN: 0 7445 4372 X

Something Else
Author: Kathryn Cave
Illustrator: Chris Riddell
Publisher: Puffin Books (1995)
ISBN: 0 14 054907 2

Slow Loris
Author and illustrator: Alexis Deacon
Publisher: Red Fox Picture Books (2003)
ISBN: 0 09 941426 0

The Smartest Giant in Town
Author: Julia Donaldson
Illustrator: Axel Scheffler
Publisher: Macmillan Children's Books (2002)
ISBN: 0 333 96396 2

Katie Morag Delivers the Mail
Author and illustrator: Mairi Hedderwick
Publisher: Red Fox Picture Books (1984)
ISBN: 0 09 922072 5

Amazing Grace
Author: Mary Hoffman
Illustrator: Caroline Binch
Publisher: Frances Lincoln Ltd (1991)
ISBN: 0 7112 0699 6

Dogger
Author and illustrator: Shirley Hughes
Publisher: Red Fox Picture Books (1993)
ISBN: 0 09 992790 X

CLASSROOM AND HOME MATERIALS

All Join In

TOPICS

✓ *Living with siblings*

✓ *Helping others*

✓ *Making the most of every day*

✓ *Using our imagination*

✓ *Being part of a family*

SUMMARY

This is a book of poems about families joining in activities with each other. It is perfect for reading aloud. Lots of quacks, beeps, clangs and bongs!

TALKING POINTS

'All Join In' (first poem)

• Take turns to add the sound effects as you read each part of the poem.

• Do you think it really is a lovely sound when Sandra plays the trumpet?

• When everyone joins in with the music, what instruments do you see? (You might need to do some research to help with this.)

• What do you feel is wonderful about Amy's tantrum?

• Why do you think she is having a tantrum?

• What sorts of things have you had a tantrum about? Did it help?

• Why do you think Bernard kicked the dustbin?

• What other noises can be loud but fun?

• How do you think Mum is feeling?

• What clues are there to this?

'Sliding'

• Use your imagination to think what else the banisters could be.

• How could you use an armchair to imagine doing something exciting?

'All Join In' (second poem)

• Which of the activities are fun and which would we normally see as chores?

• Look closely at the pictures. What is each individual doing?

• Look closely at the animals in the pictures. How is each one feeling?

• In each scene, why is it a good thing if everyone joins in?

• What activities at school are better if we all join in? (Examples are playing games at break time, tidying up the classroom, sorting out the library.)

• Think about some activities that we all do together as a school. Do we celebrate special days/weeks? (Examples are book week, Red Nose Day, science week.)

• Think about our school traditions. Is there a school song? Is there a special way we greet new teachers or pupils? Do we have leaving ceremonies?

• Can you think of a new school tradition that it would be a good idea to start?

Author and illustrator: Quentin Blake
Publisher: Red Fox Picture Books (1992)   ISBN: 0 09 996470 8

CIRCLE-TIME SUGGESTIONS

In 'Sliding', the children imagine the banisters are an elephant's trunk and a mountainside. Pass an ordinary classroom object around the circle and ask the children to imagine what else it could become. They could mime the object they have in mind and see if others could guess what it is. (For example, a pencil could be a magic wand, half of a pair of chopsticks, a tiny javelin.) Change objects when they run out of ideas.

Sentence stem

'Something it is better to do together is . . .'

If you want to explore their choices more deeply, you could ask some of the children to explain what they said.

Extension

The following two questions can be used as stimuli for further rounds and discussions:

- **What activities are more fun with friends or family?**

- **What chores are easier to do when everyone joins in?**

FOLLOW-UP ACTIVITIES

- **Work together or in small groups to write a poem(s) about all the things you enjoy doing as a class. Base the poem(s) on the structure of 'All Join In' (first or second poem). The new poem(s) could be displayed in the classroom, performed in assembly or included in a class anthology. Add actions and sound effects to create a dramatic reading and have a great deal of fun.**

- **Play Grab and Run with a small group. This can be done to music. Choose a few children to take part. Other children can have a go on another occasion. Walk round the classroom at the head of the group, who have formed a line behind you, picking up things that need tidying away. Pass the first item behind you to the child who is next in line, telling them where it needs to go. That child grabs it and runs to put it away in the correct place. They then return and join the back of the line. This process is repeated until all the items are in their correct places. There is usually some competition about who is the fastest at getting back to the end of the line after tidying up their item.**

ASSEMBLY IDEA

Perform your class 'All Join In' poem(s) to the whole school, with sound effects, actions or musical instruments as appropriate.

Involve the whole school in making an 'All Join In' display. Cover the display with photographs of people in school doing things together. (Examples are presenting assemblies together, dressing up for Red Nose Day, making music together, reading together, building models, participating in sports day, taking part in chess tournaments, going on school trips, eating Christmas lunch.) This can be a very positive focal point for the school.

All Join In

BOOK DETAILS

Author and illustrator:
Quentin Blake

Publisher: Red Fox Picture
Books (1992)

ISBN: 0 09 996470 8

TOPICS

✓ *Living with siblings*

✓ *Helping others*

✓ *Making the most of*
every day

✓ *Using our imagination*

✓ *Being part of a family*

SUMMARY

This is a book of poems about
families joining in activities with
each other. It is perfect for reading
aloud. Lots of quacks, beeps, clangs
and bongs!

THINGS TO TALK ABOUT

- Look at the picture on the cover. What is each person doing?
  How are they feeling?

- Read some or all of the poems together. Make sure you make the noises loud.

- Which poem would each of you choose as your favourite, and why?

- Many of the poems are about looking on the bright side of things. In 'Nice
  Weather for Ducks' the family looks on the bright side of rainy weather. Can
  you think of things that are good about windy weather? Snowy weather?

- In 'Sliding', we find another good thing about rainy weather: the games you
  can play inside. What do you do together when the weather is bad?

- What else could you do when the weather is bad?

- In the first 'All Join In' poem, different people's talents are celebrated. What
  special talents do each member of your family have?

- Look at the second 'All Join In' poem. All of the activities are plainly done
  regularly by all of the family together. What activities do you do together at home?

- In the second 'All Join In' poem, jobs are made easier by doing them together.
  What jobs could you do together at home that you don't already do that way?

THINGS TO DO OR MAKE

Make a rainy-day box to keep your child entertained whilst the weather is bad. It could contain colouring pencils, story tapes, dressing-up clothes, a cookery book and puzzle books. It is very important that this box comes out only on rainy days so it remains special. You can change or add items to the box to keep it fresh and exciting. Ask your children for suggestions about what to include.

Make a poster for each person in the house, illustrating their special talents. You can write, draw and include photographs.

Find a space where a jigsaw can be left out until it is completed. You can all work on it at the same time, or do a little bit whenever you pass. Make sure you all admire it when it is finished. Then try another one.

You could introduce some tidy-up traditions like the ones below so that everyone can join in:

> *The first game is called Grab and Run. This can be done to music. Your child may be familiar with it from school but it works well at home too. You walk at the head of a line of people in your home, picking up objects that need to be tidied up. Pass the first item behind you to the next person in line. As you pass it to the person behind you, tell them where the object belongs. They grab it and run to put it away. They then come back and join the back of the line. There is usually some competition about who is the quickest at getting back to the end of the line.*

> *The second tradition is called Hit the House. This is especially helpful when you are overwhelmed by the mess in the bedrooms. Again, you can do this to music. The owner of the first bedroom to be tidied sits on their bed and directs cleaning-up operations. They don't have to do any work in their own bedroom. You then move on to the next bedroom, where the owner of the first bedroom becomes a member of the work party, and the owner of the second bedroom directs proceedings. You could promise a treat at the end when all the bedrooms are tidy.*

Invent other family traditions. Traditions are often good glue to hold a family together. For example:

> *Choose a favourite song to sing. Make sure everybody knows all of the words. It doesn't have to be a children's song, just one you all enjoy.*

> *Have birthday traditions or ones associated with particular religious festivals. Some families have the Birthday Fairy, who fills the birthday person's bedroom with fairy lights and balloons.*

> *Decorate the tree together just before Christmas, if you celebrate this festival. Buy or make together a new decoration each year, to add to your collection.*

> *Have a regular outing to a favourite place, one where everybody knows they will find something to enjoy when they get there. This does not have to be somewhere expensive. It could be the local park, perhaps with a picnic to add to the fun.*

Mister Magnolia

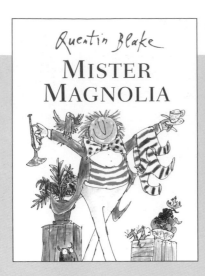

TOPICS

✓ *Friendship and belonging*

✓ *Making the most of every day*

✓ *Using our imagination*

SUMMARY OF STORY

Mr Magnolia does not have a very comfortable life. He has pesky parakeets, his house has packing-case furniture and he has an enormous pet dinosaur to feed. Owls keep him awake at night and, worst of all, he does not even have a pair of boots. However, he is the happiest chap you could imagine! He dances to his sisters' music, he is good to his friends and he makes the best of everything in his life. But he would like a second boot so he can go out and play in the rain. When he is finally given a wonderful boot by one of his friends, he is ecstatic, even though it doesn't match the boot he already has. He immediately goes out to play in the puddles with all of his friends.

TALKING POINTS

- What are the good things in Mr Magnolia's life?

- What are the not-so-good things?

- Describe what Mr Magnolia is wearing on the first page. What do you think of his clothes?

- Look at Mr Magnolia's face in each picture. How does it show what he is feeling?

- Look at each picture and ask the children how they would feel if they were in that situation.

- What books do you think Mr Magnolia has on his bedside table on the page where he is listening to his owls learning to hoot?

- What do you think Mr Magnolia's medals are for on the page where he salutes the mice?

- What is the one thing that bothers Mr Magnolia more than anything else?

- Who solves this problem for him?

- Is the new boot a perfect match for the one he already has? Does this seem to bother Mr Magnolia? Why not?

- Where do you think Mr Magnolia's friend got the boot?

- Where might the other boot of the pair be?

- What is the first thing Mr Magnolia does with his new boot?

MOTION FOR DEBATE

'This class believes that people will like and respect you more if you dress well.'

Mr Magnolia has holes in his suit and only one boot. If he were a child at school, he would be told to smarten up. However, he exemplifies many characteristics that we would like to see in our children – for example friendliness, cheerfulness, kindness and generosity. He also has lots of friends who love him dearly.

Author and illustrator: Quentin Blake
Publisher: Red Fox Picture Books (1999)   ISBN: 0 09 940042 1

CIRCLE-TIME SUGGESTIONS

Mr Magnolia knows how to live. He makes the best of everything and is full of life and love for his friends. Mr Magnolia doesn't cry or complain or blame. He is selfless and generous hearted. He is a glass-half-full person! As a result, he has lots of friends who love him as much as he loves them.

Ask the children to think about things in their school lives that do not seem to be quite perfect. Get them to complete a sentence by adding something that they find annoying or isn't as they would wish to the following stem:

'One thing I don't like in my school life is . . .'

Now ask the class to brainstorm ways to make some of these blights into blessings. You might need to do this over a number of sessions to cover everybody's issues.

You might want to make it clear that this circle time is about everyday niggles rather than potentially more sensitive matters. You could tell the class that they can come and see you later if they have anything more private that they would like to share. You should refer to your school's child protection procedures to find out how to handle any serious disclosures.

FOLLOW-UP ACTIVITIES

• Put all of your blights and blessings on a display board. Try to include photographs of how the children could be blessings to help to correct the blights. Use a digital camera if you have access to one.

• You might like to read other stories and poems about how to have a good time in a simple way. Peter Dixon's 'The Colour of My Dreams' in *The Colour of My Dreams and Other Poems*, published by Macmillan Children's Books (2002), is good for this.

• Get the video or DVD of *Shrek* out of a public library, or borrow a copy from someone in your class, and watch some of it together. Choose an excerpt that focuses on the differences between how one or more of the characters appear outwardly and how they really are. You might like to have a discussion about how the outside of a person is not always a good reflection of how they are on the inside.

ASSEMBLY IDEA

Introduce the school to your work on moving from blights to blessings. Let your class tell them about some they looked at. See what other classes can come up with. You could share these ideas in subsequent assemblies or on display boards round the school.

Mister Magnolia

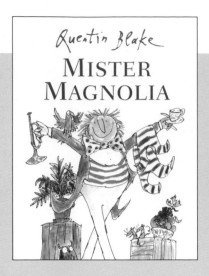

BOOK DETAILS

Author and illustrator: Quentin Blake

Publisher: Red Fox Picture Books (1999)

ISBN: 0 09 940042 1

TOPICS

✓ *Friendship and belonging*

✓ *Making the most of every day*

✓ *Using our imagination*

SUMMARY OF STORY

Mr Magnolia does not have a very comfortable life. He has pesky parakeets, his house has packing-case furniture and he has an enormous pet dinosaur to feed. Owls keep him awake at night and, worst of all, he does not even have a pair of boots. However, he is the happiest chap you could imagine! He dances to his sisters' music, he is good to his friends and he makes the best of everything in his life. But he would like a second boot so he can go out and play in the rain. When he is finally given a wonderful boot by one of his friends, he is ecstatic, even though it doesn't match the boot he already has. He immediately goes out to play in the puddles with all of his friends.

THINGS TO THINK ABOUT

Mr Magnolia knows how to live. He makes the best of everything and is full of life and love for his friends. Mr Magnolia doesn't cry or complain or blame. He is selfless and generous hearted. He is a glass-half-full person! As a result, he has lots of friends who love him as much as he loves them.

THINGS TO TALK ABOUT

- Does Mr Magnolia have a comfortable life?

- How would you describe his life?

- Can you tell from the pictures that Mr Magnolia's trumpet is old? What clues are you given regarding this?

- In what ways do you think Mr Magnolia's sisters are 'lovely'?

- What does Mr Magnolia think about their flute playing? How do you know this from the story?

- Go through the book and look at all of Mr Magnolia's activities. Does he do many of them on his own?

- Why doesn't he have a bicycle?

- What is the best way to ride a scooter with one boot?

- Can you take more friends for rides on a bike or a scooter?

- Who is on Mr Magnolia's scooter?

- Find the little mice throughout the book. How do you know they are his friends? Which pages show us they are his friends?

- Look at the expressions on the faces of the people in the book. How many people are smiling? When do they smile? Why is this in each picture?

- Find the only page where Mr Magnolia looks really unhappy.

- Why can't he go out in the rain?

- What does Mr Magnolia's friend give him?

- Is her gift a fancy boot? Does it match his other boot?

- How do you know what Mr Magnolia thinks of his gift?

- What does Mr Magnolia do as soon as he can go out?

- That night he goes to sleep really happy. (Look at the smile on his face!)

THINGS TO DO OR MAKE

You can play Blight to Blessing with your child. Ask them to think of things they don't like (blights) and then to find ways to make them into blessings. For example:

Blight: *I have to share a room with my brother. (Who's a bit of a blighter!)*

Blessing: *We can tell each other stories at night. We can use torches to make shadows in the dark and guess what they are. We can have huge rolled-up-sock wars, which you could join in with. (Oh, go on! Throw yourself into it! Build defences, stockpile several pairs, go for a massive attack, and tire everyone out.)*

Blight: *It's a wet Saturday in March.*

Blessing: *We can plant seeds in pots or clean yoghurt pots, and soon they will grow.*

Blight: *We have to walk home from school.*

Blessing: *We can pretend to be bears as we walk. We can sing songs. We can tell each other about our day. We can try to get a ride on the back of the buggy.*

Blight: *It's Sunday and it's raining.*

Blessing: *We can explore the cupboard under the stairs, or another interesting cupboard, to see what we can find. We can turn the sofa into a den. We can make scrambled eggs on toast for tea.*

You could make a record of the blessings in a scrapbook, possibly with accompanying photographs. This can be used as a reference book if the blights raise their heads again another day.

Alfie Weather

TOPICS

✓ *Living with siblings*

✓ *Making the most of every day*

✓ *Using our imagination*

✓ *Being part of a family*

SUMMARY

This is a book of stories and poems about Alfie and his family. Each one values the small details of family life and treasures life's everyday events. In 'A Journey to the North Pole', Alfie and his sister Annie Rose play with Grandma. Although it is a rainy day, they have a wonderful time going on outdoor and indoor expeditions.

TALKING POINTS

'A Journey to the North Pole'

- Why does Alfie get cross with Annie Rose?

- Is she really trying to annoy him?

- Have you ever had a similar problem with a brother, sister or friend?

- What do Alfie and his sister enjoy about walking in the rain? What are the drawbacks?

- Look at the pictures of Alfie, Annie Rose and Grandma on their walk. How would you feel if you were there with them?

- How were Alfie and his sister getting along at the start of the story? Why do you think this?

- Look at the pictures of them on the indoor expedition. How are they getting along now?

- Why do you think things have changed?

- How do Alfie and Annie Rose use their imagination in each of the rooms that they visit?

- How does Grandma cope with the day?

- Does she ever get cross? What does she do instead?

- Look at the picture of the attic. What can you see that has been stored there?

- Look at the language used to describe the indoor expedition. Pick out the words that are descriptive – for example *billowing, dense, fast-flowing* – and particular to expeditions – like *Base Camp*. How does this language enhance the children's play?

Author and illustrator: Shirley Hughes
Publisher: Red Fox Picture Books (2002)   ISBN: 0 09 940425 7

CIRCLE-TIME SUGGESTIONS

This can be a good time to talk about the highs and lows of life with brothers and sisters. You could ask children to share what they enjoy about having siblings and what they find a challenge. This needs to be handled carefully and is best suited to a general discussion, as you may have some only children in your group. Use your discretion.

Sentence stem

'When it is too wet to play outside I like to . . .'

Wet weather can be a problem for children who find it hard to think of games to play. Try to encourage the children to be inventive with the ideas they share so that they don't talk entirely about watching DVDs or playing video games.

FOLLOW-UP ACTIVITIES

• In groups, tell the children to plan expeditions around the school grounds, using their imagination to turn them into a new exciting place – for example, a jungle, a desert or a pirate ship.

• On an outline of the school grounds, draw a map of the imaginary place – for example, convert the slide into a mountain.

• Name the different features of the map – for example, The Craggy Mountain of Doom – and add other descriptive words from their group talk.

• Take the whole class outside, and get each group to lead the class on their expedition following their map.

• Encourage the whole class to role-play the story of the expedition. You could do this over several days. Ask the children to imagine what they would pack for the journey. They could draw or write their provisions list.

• Ask the children to talk in their groups about the imaginary place, using descriptive language to make the place come alive.

What dangers might they encounter?

What will they see, hear, smell and feel?

Encourage the children to create the story of their expedition in writing or using artwork.

• There is a photocopiable sheet on page 105 to send home with the 'For home' resources for this book.

Alfie Weather

BOOK DETAILS

Author and illustrator: Shirley Hughes

Publisher: Red Fox Picture Books (2002)

ISBN: 0 09 940425 7

TOPICS

✓ *Living with siblings*

✓ *Making the most of every day*

✓ *Using our imagination*

✓ *Being part of a family*

SUMMARY

This is a book of stories and poems about Alfie and his family. Each one values the small details of family life and treasures life's everyday events. In 'A Journey to the North Pole', Alfie and his sister Annie Rose play with Grandma. Although it is a rainy day, they have a wonderful time going on outdoor and indoor expeditions.

THINGS TO TALK ABOUT

• What games/activities do you like doing with your brother/sister? What would you rather do on your own?

• Why does Annie Rose keep trying to join in with what Alfie is doing? Is she doing it to annoy him?

• How does Grandma distract the children?

• Was she very brave to go outside in the rainy weather?

• Do you think anybody complained about going out in the rain?

• What can we wear to make going out in the rain fun?

• Alfie and Annie Rose went to the North Pole in Grandma's attic. Grandma encouraged them to use their imagination to change everyday objects into exciting places and things. What adventures did they have on the way? Look carefully at each page.

• What objects can you see in the picture of Grandma's attic?

• Look at the treasure that Alfie and Annie Rose find. What can you see?

• What piece of treasure would you keep from their collection?

• Why did you choose it?

• What other games might Alfie and Annie Rose have played with the treasure?

• What did they do with the treasure when the sun came out?

• How do you think Alfie and Annie Rose felt after their expedition? Do you think they were tired?

THINGS TO DO OR MAKE

Go on an imaginative journey. You might turn the sofa into a pirate ship, or imagine that a cardboard box is a racing car (no need to decorate it – children have good imaginations), or use sheets to make a den under a table and pretend that it is an igloo.

If you can get outside, go on a similar expedition around your garden or a nearby park – trees can be giants, bushes can be a jungle.

Go on a treasure hunt! You could fill an old ice-cream tub with corks and curtain rings covered in foil and then hide it somewhere outside. Try using the rules of Hunt the Thimble to guide your child. Use the treasure map template included in these resources to plan a route to the treasure.

It is really important that you take part in any such role play. Don't worry about your acting skills – no one will be interested in what you are up to.

Trash or treasure. Alfie and Annie Rose enjoyed looking at things in Grandma's attic. Find a box from your attic or a store cupboard and look through it together. Throw out the rubbish (or, if suitable, take items down to the local charity shop), keep the treasure. Talk about the history of some of the things you find.

Rose's box. Make up a story about an imaginary person who might have lived in your home. Now make them a treasure box. Take a little cardboard box or tin, and fill it with items you find at home. You can put everything back at the end of the day. When we played this we imagined someone from about 1910. We called her Rose and we put into a box some rose-scented soap, two hair ribbons, an old photograph in a frame, roses from the garden, an old pair of lace gloves, and a letter that we wrote. We imagined it was a letter from Rose's sister describing a journey she had taken. We rubbed a used teabag on the letter and aged it in the oven.

Rain walk. Walking in the rain can be fun, especially if you are wearing the right clothes. Put on your boots, coats and hats and go out for a wet and splashy walk. Who can find the biggest puddles to jump in?

Grandfather's Pencil and the Room of Stories

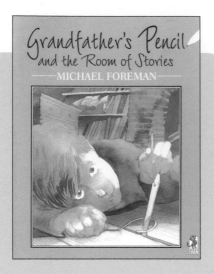

Grandfather's Pencil
and the Room of Stories
—MICHAEL FOREMAN—

TOPICS

✓ *Being part of a family*

✓ *Valuing special things*

✓ *Valuing memories*

SUMMARY OF STORY

As a boy sleeps, a pencil tells its story – how it started as part of a very tall tree and went on to live in a box with other pencils. The paper, the table, the door and the floorboards go on to tell their stories too. When the boy grows up, he shares his memories with his grandson Jack, who lives in his grandfather's old house. Jack goes home to find his grandfather's pencil hidden under the floorboards.

TALKING POINTS

- Look at the first few pages of the story. How can you tell if the boy lives in the present day or not?

- Many of the objects in the boy's room have a story to tell, a memory to share. How do the objects feel about their memories? Pick out the words that demonstrate the strength of their feelings.

- What would be the memories of some of the objects in your bedroom?

- What are your own memories? What are the important events in the story of your life so far?

- Memories can make us feel happy, sad, excited or proud. How do you feel about some of your memories?

- The boy in the story has 'far to go'. Where do you think you might go in your life?

- Where do you think you will be in twenty years' time?

- Jack enjoys listening to his grandfather's stories about his life on the sea. What sort of stories might he have told Jack?

- Do you know any of your parents' or grandparents' memories? Which do you like best?

- Compare the picture of the city in Jack's day with the picture of the city when his grandfather was a boy. What differences can you see? Has anything remained the same?

- Do you own anything that used to belong to someone else? What do you know about it?

CIRCLE-TIME SUGGESTIONS

Play Kim's Game with a tray of objects, including some of those mentioned in the book. Show the tray of objects to the children in the circle, cover the tray and then remove an object. Keep this object hidden under the cloth as you remove it from the tray. Ask the children what object has been removed. Repeat this, allowing different children to remove objects in the same way.

Sentence stem

Circle times are a good opportunity to share valued and important memories. Use the sentence stem below for this activity. Having a store of happy memories is useful for a child to draw on when life is difficult.

'One of my favourite memories is . . .'

Author and illustrator: Michael Foreman
Publisher: Red Fox Picture Books (1995)   ISBN: 0 09 950331 X

FOLLOW-UP ACTIVITIES

• Plot the journey of the piece of paper – from the seed to the tree, to the logs to the paper mill, to the shop to the boy's bedroom, out of the window, over the city, into the tree and into the birds' nests. This journey could be drawn as a timeline or used as the basis for a story or poem.

• Ask the children to draw or write about where they think they will go in their lives. This could be a single sentence/picture or a number of sentences/pictures explaining different ambitions. This list of hopes and dreams can be used to give children a purpose for tackling difficult school work.

• Draw or write about the memories of the pencil's companions under the floorboards. What is the history of the bent pin, the old gold coin and the whale-bone button?

• Make a class museum – either use objects from home whose history is known or everyday objects and invent the history. Write a museum card for each object, explaining its history.

• Make Paper Bag Trails. Start with a paper bag. Pin it onto a noticeboard. Now imagine something that might have been in the bag – plums, for example – and tell its story. At each stage find a relevant picture to put on the board and encourage someone to write a piece. If you can find relevant artefacts, pin those to the wall as well – for example, plum-tree leaves, blossom, labels from plum-jam jars. For example, the story may start with a plum stone in the earth, then a tree growing tall and strong in a beautiful orchard. Subsequently we see the blossom in the warm sun smelling of spring and early summer, and then move on to the cheerful pickers up ladders. We may then see a journey by lorry to the wholesale market, and the sights and smells of the market. Finally we see the plums lying in a box outside a shop in a city. In the next box lie piles of okra or lychees – and there is the start of another paper bag trail!

Grandfather's Pencil and the Room of Stories

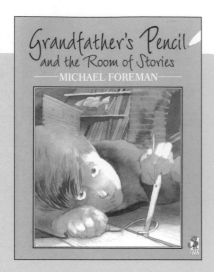

BOOK DETAILS

Author and illustrator:
Michael Foreman

Publisher: Red Fox Picture
Books (1995)

ISBN: 0 09 950331 X

TOPICS

✓ *Being part of a family*

✓ *Valuing special things*

✓ *Valuing memories*

SUMMARY OF STORY

As a boy sleeps, a pencil tells its story – how it started as part of a very tall tree and went on to live in a box with other pencils. The paper, the table, the door and the floorboards go on to tell their stories too. When the boy grows up, he shares his memories with his grandson Jack, who lives in his grandfather's old house. Jack goes home to find his grandfather's pencil hidden under the floorboards.

THINGS TO THINK ABOUT

• What memories would you like to pass on to your child?

• What objects do you own that used to belong to someone in your family?

THINGS TO TALK ABOUT

• What stories do the objects in the boy's room have to tell?

• What are your memories? What are the important events in the story of your life so far?

• Memories can make us feel happy, sad, excited and proud. How do you feel about some of your memories?

• What do you think you will do in the future?

• What will you have to do to get there?

• Jack's grandfather tells him stories about his life on the sea. What stories do you think he told him?

• Share some family memories. What events do you all remember? (Examples are a favourite holiday, a special day, funny or sad events from the past.)

• Share events from your own life or from the lives of their grandparents with your child. You could compare school experiences, favourite toys, music and so on.

• Jack is excited to find his grandfather's pencil. Tell your child about something you own that was passed down to you by someone else. What is its history? It might be a valuable family heirloom or something simple like the pencil. Either way, its history will make it special.

THINGS TO DO OR MAKE

Talk to your child's grandparents about their memories. Look through old photograph albums and find out about the stories behind the pictures.

Find out about your family history. Does your family have roots in another part of the UK or in another country? Do you know the names of your great-grandparents? Great-great-grandparents? Do you know what jobs they did?

Look online at www.nationalarchives.gov.uk. This website has some guidance on how to get started.

Go hunting for treasure. It is amazing what you can find down the back of the sofa, under the bed and behind the chest of drawers. See what you can find together. Perhaps you will find something with a story behind it, or perhaps you can make up a story for each object.

If you want to be certain of finding treasure, you might want to hide something interesting in advance. You may live in the sort of home that is filled with old books, photographs, furniture or clothes, or you may live in the sort of home where the oldest thing in it is you! If the latter, take a trip to a charity shop, hunt about for something old that costs only a few pence: a chipped plate, a cracked vase, an odd knife or spoon, anything old enough to have a history.

If you have most of your photographs on the computer, you might like to print a few of them and make a small, keepsake photograph album with your child. You could write a little piece about the story behind each photograph.

Down the Dragon's Tongue

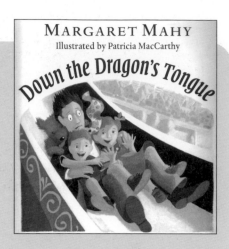

TOPICS

✓ *Worries and fears*

✓ *Making the most of every day*

✓ *Being part of a family*

✓ *Making choices*

✓ *Exploring reputation*

SUMMARY OF STORY

Mr Prospero is a very neat and tidy father who behaves extremely sensibly until his children introduce him to a slide called the Dragon's Tongue. To the amazement of his family and himself, Mr Prospero discovers a wilder side to his character.

TALKING POINTS

- Does Mr Prospero look happy in his office? If so, why do you think he is happy there?

- Does Mr Prospero look neat and tidy? Is his hair tidy? Describe his tie.

- Does he look quite so happy when he gets home? If not, why do you think that is?

- Is his home quiet?

- What do the twins want to do?

- The sign in Mr Prospero's office says 'You can do it! You can do it!' What do you think this means for him at work?

- In the office he can always 'do it'. What does he find it difficult to do in the park? Why do you think this is?

- What do the twins say to make him go down the slide with them?

- Look at Mr Prospero's face when he first goes down the slide. Does he look the boss of this situation?

- What happens to Mr Prospero as he goes down the slide a third time? Look at his hair and tie now.

- When he goes down the slide the next time, what does he do? Is that really a sensible thing to do?

- When he gets home, what does Mr Prospero look like?

- How is he different from the way he looks and acts at the start of the story?

- What difficult thing has Mr Prospero discovered he can do?

- How do you think he will behave from now on?

MOTION FOR DEBATE

'This class believes that it is a good thing to take risks and do wild things.'

Author: Margaret Mahy   Illustrator: Patricia MacCarthy
Publisher: Frances Lincoln Ltd (2001)   ISBN: 0 7112 1617 7

CIRCLE-TIME SUGGESTIONS

We all feel fearful at different times, and about different things. Using the sentence stem below will help the children to realise that they are not alone in feeling fearful every now and then:

'I get a bit scared when I have to . . .'

Extension

You might like to explore this issue further by asking the children to think of things that have helped them when they have felt scared. If someone helped, what did they do that was helpful?

FOLLOW-UP ACTIVITIES

Mr Prospero had to step out of his comfort zone when he went on the Dragon's Tongue. Talk to the children about things they find difficult to face. What are their dragon's tongues? (For example, going on the adventure playground equipment, being in a play, speaking in a big voice in circle time, having a part in the class assembly.)

On a noticeboard put a big sign just like the one in Mr Prospero's office, that says:

We can do it!

We can do it!

Now draw a wide dragon's tongue right across the middle of the board. You could copy the one in the storybook, but make it very wide.

Help the children to think of things they find a challenge, or use the examples they gave in the circle time. You could use a digital camera to take photographs of the children having a go at facing their dragon's tongues throughout the week. Put the photographs on the dragon's tongue.

See how many children can slide down the dragon's tongue by meeting their challenge during the week. Celebrate their achievements as an encouragement to those children still working on their dragon's tongues.

This activity should be a positive experience for all the children. Careful handling of the choice of difficulties is necessary.

Down the Dragon's Tongue

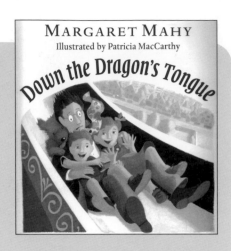

BOOK DETAILS

Author: Margaret Mahy

Illustrator: Patricia MacCarthy

Publisher: Frances Lincoln Ltd (2001)

ISBN: 0 7112 1617 7

TOPICS

✓ *Worries and fears*

✓ *Making the most of every day*

✓ *Being part of a family*

✓ *Making choices*

✓ *Exploring reputation*

SUMMARY OF STORY

Mr Prospero is a very neat and tidy father who behaves extremely sensibly until his children introduce him to a slide called the Dragon's Tongue. To the amazement of his family and himself, Mr Prospero discovers a wilder side to his character.

THINGS TO THINK ABOUT

Although this is ostensibly a story for children, it carries a far bigger message for adults. Mr Prospero is a man who feels in control when he is at work, where he is sure he can rise to his own challenge of 'You can do it!' However, when he gets home the challenges of wild childhood unnerve him. He is not at all sure that he can 'do it'.

Many adults find work a nice, safe, predictable and tidy place, where they feel comfortable and in control. They often feel that home is a noisy, messy, unpredictable place, and there they may sometimes feel a failure.

The Dragon's Tongue is, of course, a metaphor. Letting go of our controlled grown-up self and deciding to throw ourselves wholeheartedly into family life – with all of its fears and losses of dignity – is like sliding down the Dragon's Tongue. It is scary.

Look at Mr Prospero's face at the beginning of the book and at the end. In both he is smiling. On the last page showing him, however, he looks truly alive. He has discovered that even though he let go of his symbols of control – his suit, his tidy hair and his shoes – he can still feel a success. He can still 'do it'.

THINGS TO TALK ABOUT

- Look at Mr Prospero in his office. How does he look? What sort of smile does he have?

- Why doesn't he look very happy when he gets home?

- Look at the pictures of him throughout the book. How does his face change?

- What does he say to himself when he gets scared in the park? What makes him scared in the park?

- What do the children say to make him climb the steps to the Dragon's Tongue?

- Once he has braved the slide and he starts to enjoy himself, he starts to take risks. Does he slide in a dangerous way?

- Look at his clothes and hair in the last picture of him. Compare them to how he looked when he arrived in the park. What do you notice?

- Who helped Mr Prospero be brave?

- Is Mr Prospero the same sort of dad at the end of the book as he was at the beginning?

- Is he a better dad at the end of the book? Why do you think that?

Sometimes we feel we will hang onto our authority only if we hang onto our dignity. Do you think Mr Prospero suffered any loss of authority in his home and with his children after he conquered his fear of the Dragon's Tongue?

Do you think a man in a fruit salad tie always has a hidden wild side?

THINGS TO DO OR MAKE

Work out a few things that might be dragon's tongues for you as a parent:

Do you feel uncomfortable when the house gets messy during wild games?

Do you find it embarrassing to join in a game of Let's Pretend? (For example, sitting under the table being a pirate.)

Do you find doing funny voices when you read the bedtime story embarrassing, even though there are no other adults there to hear you?

Being a parent is just as much a job as anything that happens outside the home. Give yourself permission to throw yourself into the dafter, jollier side of parenting – you can do it!

Talk to your child about what may be their dragon's tongue. You could talk about how Mr Prospero felt at the top of the slide compared to how he felt at the bottom, and how this changed as he had more goes.

With your child, you could write a list of 'Ways to defeat the dragon' – strategies that your child could use when they face their dragon's tongue. For example, if your child is going to try to go to sleep without their light on, the strategies could include these:

Start with a small lamp on.

Try it with a small plug-in night light.

Keep a little torch nearby for your child to use in emergencies.

Stick on the ceiling some glow-in-the-dark stars and planets that can only be seen without the light on.

Have a cuddly toy for your child to tell their worries to, and explain it will look after them when there is no light on. It could be a toy that is a nocturnal animal, one that will only come out when it is dark.

Check with your child how they are getting along as they will need your help and encouragement. Mr Prospero had to have help and to make a few attempts before he started to enjoy himself. Once your child is managing their dragon's tongue on a regular basis, you could share in a small treat together. Try to agree what this is before your child starts work on the problem, so that they have something to work towards and look forward to.

Owl Babies

TOPICS

✓ *Worries and fears*

✓ *Living with siblings*

✓ *Missing Mum*

SUMMARY OF STORY

Sarah, Percy and Bill, three little owls, wake up one night to find their Owl Mother gone. They go outside and sit and think. Where is their Owl Mother? What is she doing? Is she safe? Will she come home again? In time, their Owl Mother does return, much to the little owls' joy!

TALKING POINTS

- How can you tell that these are baby owls? Look at their colour and size compared to the Owl Mother.

- The owl babies for most of the story are really worried. Which are the pages where they are truly happy? Why do you think this is?

- When they discover that their Owl Mother is missing, what do the little owls do?

- What do they think about?

- Is thinking always better than crying? (This is quite a difficult question and it should be given plenty of discussion time. You might prefer to use it as a motion for debate.)

- Does little Bill think? Is he a bit too young to think in the same way as Sarah and Percy?

- They go outside to wait for their Owl Mother. What are the good and bad things about this idea?

- How do the little owls start to feel when their Owl Mother still doesn't come home?

- What do they start to think then? What sort of scary thoughts do you think come into their minds?

- What things might be moving in the woods around the little owls?

- Do they cry and shout and make a big fuss when their Owl Mother doesn't come home? What do they do instead?

- What do they do when she does come home?

- What does their Owl Mother say?

- Do you sometimes feel like the owl babies when you are left at school in the morning?

- Do you always do what the owl babies do? Do you think? Or do you sometimes panic?

- What else could you do? (You could talk to your teacher if you feel very upset. They could help you to think and remember when the person who dropped you off said they would be back. You could think about where they said they would be. You could think about what they might be doing now. You could think about the end of the school day. Do you ever get left at school all night?)

Author: Martin Waddell   Illustrator: Patrick Benson
Publisher: Walker Books Ltd (1994)   ISBN: 0 7445 3167 5

CIRCLE-TIME SUGGESTIONS

On page 106 is a poem called 'Morning School'.
The poem can be used to explore feelings children
may have when they are dropped off at school.
This can be quite upsetting for young children, and
some older ones too. The poem offers reassurance
and a window on someone else's experience
that mirrors their own. Such connections have a
positive impact on an upset child's feelings.

Talk to the children about some of the things their
parents do when they are at school (for example:
go to work; see Grandma; go shopping; look after
the baby; clean the house; visit luxury spas for
manicures, pedicures and hot stone treatments – in
their dreams).

Sentence stem

'While I am here I think my mummy/daddy is . . .'

FOLLOW-UP ACTIVITIES

• Go through the owl babies' story. Transpose it by
retelling the story so that the owl babies become
children who are at school and miss their mum.
Change the details – for example, their mother has
gone to work instead of hunting.

• Make pictograms or visual timetables of an
imaginary child's day and an imaginary mum's/
dad's day alongside each other. If possible, take
photographs of a child and an adult not known to
your class doing various activities, and use them in
this exercise. Start with a picture of a child holding
their parent's hand. They should look as if they are
happy together.

• Home and school diaries. Create a diary template
that can be used by children and parents to share
information about their day. It might work well to
have the child template down one side of a folded
piece of A4 paper, with the adult template facing it.
For younger children, the template
might have spaces for pictures of a
favourite morning activity, what
they had for lunch and a favourite
afternoon activity. For older
children, there could be sentence
starts – for example: This morning I
enjoyed . . .; For lunch I ate . . .;
This afternoon I . . .; Tomorrow I am
looking forward to . . . The child
could complete their half of the
diary in school, then take the sheet
home for a parent to complete the
other half.

• There is a photocopiable sheet on
page 107 to send home with the
'For home' resources for this book.

Owl Babies

BOOK DETAILS

Author: Martin Waddell

Illustrator: Patrick Benson

Publisher: Walker Books Ltd (1994)

ISBN: 0 7445 3167 5

TOPICS

✓ *Worries and fears*

✓ *Living with siblings*

✓ *Missing Mum*

SUMMARY OF STORY

Sarah, Percy and Bill, three little owls, wake up one night to find their Owl Mother gone. They go outside and sit and think. Where is their Owl Mother? What is she doing? Is she safe? Will she come home again? In time, their Owl Mother does return, much to the little owls' joy!

THINGS TO TALK ABOUT

- Which owl is Sarah, which Percy, and which Bill? How do you know?

- Look at the Owl Mother. Is she a different colour? Why is that?

- Show your child how big an owl is with your hands (about 35cm) and then work out how small Sarah, Percy and Bill are in comparison.

- When they find their Owl Mother is gone, what do Sarah and Percy do? What about Bill? Does he look out of their tree?

- How do you think Bill feels?

- Have you ever woken up and found that Mummy and Daddy have gone out and that there is a babysitter? Have you ever said 'I want my Mummy,' like Bill?

- What did Sarah and Percy think? Could you do that when you find Mummy and Daddy have gone out?

- What did Bill do? Did he think? Why not? Is he a bit too young to work out where his Owl Mother might be?

- The owls came out of their house. Was that a good idea or not?

- Do you sometimes get out of bed when there is a babysitter?

- Why are you safer than the owls?

- At first, Sarah and Percy seem a bit less worried than poor Bill. They keep thinking sensible thoughts about where their Owl Mother might be.

- What does Sarah say that shows us she is starting to get worried too?

- Eventually all the little owls get worried. What do they do then?

- When they close their eyes, do you think maybe the little owls go back to sleep? (Owls can sleep on branches.)

- When you are feeling upset because Mummy and Daddy are out, could you try going back to sleep? When you get back to bed you could close your eyes and go back to sleep, just like the owl babies.

- Can you see the Owl Mother coming home through the trees?

- She tells the owl babies that they need not have worried because they knew she would come home, and Sarah and Percy have a little think and say that they did know that. Bill is just happy she is home!

- Would it help if I said 'I'll be home soon – don't worry' when I go out?

THINGS TO DO OR MAKE

Talk about times when your child is left by one or both parents or carers. This may be at nursery, with a child minder or at playgroup, or even at school.

What could they do if they are worried? (Like the owl babies, they could try thinking about where you are and what you are doing, and remember that when you have finished you will come home or come to collect them.)

If they are still scared, at least they are not in a wood with no adult, like the poor owl babies. The owl babies cuddled up together. Whom or what could they cuddle or gain some reassurance from? Talk to them about this. You could say to them: 'If you are missing Mummy, then your teacher / child minder / playgroup leader would be a good person to tell. They would help you feel better.'

Use the picture of the Owl Mother and her babies included with these resources. Before you have to go out in the evening, look at this picture with your child. Talk about the baby owls in the book. Tell your child where you are going. Remind them that, like the Owl Mother in the book, you too will fly home (eventually) and that if they wake up they could talk to the babysitter and then they could go back to bed, close their eyes and think about you quietly, just like the owl babies did.

You might want to have a stuffed toy owl available so they could cuddle it and pretend it is Bill or Percy or Sarah. You could call the stuffed owl Bill or Percy or Sarah.

You might like to colour the picture of the Owl Mother and her little owls, stick it on some card, cover it with sticky-backed plastic and fix it to the fridge. If you go regularly to a certain place such as to your parents, to work or to an evening class, you could stick pictures of these places alongside the owl picture. You could then tell your child where you are going to be, showing them the photographs so they have a picture of where you are in their heads.

You could display photographs of yourself in the same way, but be aware that some children find babysitters showing them pictures of absent parents upsetting, – if that applies to your child, stick to the earlier suggestions.

The Bear under the Stairs

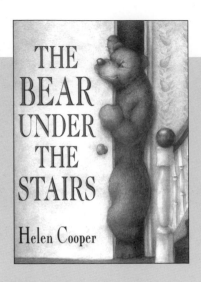

TOPICS

✓ *Worries and fears*

✓ *Sorting out problems*

✓ *Asking for help*

SUMMARY OF STORY

William is frightened of grizzly bears and of the cupboard under the stairs, where one day he thinks he sees a bear. William is worried about the bear and sneaks food to it to keep it happy. Eventually the food begins to smell and William's mum decides to do some cleaning. William admits to his fear and he and his mum tackle the problem head on.

TALKING POINTS

- Is the bear really there? To William the bear was real. All of our worries are real to us, even if they are unlikely or even impossible. Even if you have a worry that is understandable and justified, it is probably still better to face up to it.

- What are the things that William is afraid of?

- Why do you think he is frightened of these things?

- What are you frightened of? Why do you think that is?

- What does William do to try to keep the bear happy and keep his fear at bay?

- What does William think the bear looks like?

- What do you think the bear would do to William if he met him?

- How long do you think it was before William talked to anyone about his worries?

- To whom did William talk about his worries?

- To whom can you talk about your worries?

- Why didn't he talk to his mum sooner?

- How does William's mum react?

- Why was William able to be brave at last?

- What can we do to help others who are frightened or worried, even if we don't share their worries? Perhaps it would help if, like William's mother, we thought of a practical solution to the problem. Alternatively, it can help if people who are worried are distracted from obsessively thinking about their worries and fears. Is there some way we could distract a worried person? Could we play with them, go on an outing with them, or share a book?

MOTION FOR DEBATE

'This class believes that it is better to face your fears than to try to ignore them.'

In the story, William tries to manage his fears by closing his eyes and throwing food to the bear under the stairs. Would it have been better or worse if he had gone into the cupboard straightaway?

Author and illustrator: Helen Cooper
Publisher: Corgi Children's Books (1994)   ISBN: 0 552 52706 8

FOLLOW-UP ACTIVITIES

• Use a display board to create a problem page display, like the sort in magazines, but with children's problems. Collectively, or individually, write letters about the different worries that have been expressed in the circle time. Then, using the group's ideas for solutions to the worries, put up answers to the letters. You can add a few humorous solutions. You could illustrate the display board or make it look like a real page from a comic book.

• If your child has been frightened by an issue in the news, you could learn more about it from the Newsround website www.news.bbc.co.uk/cbbcnews/default.stm) or do something positive to help. Oxfam, World Vision, Tearfund, Cafod and other charities all have special resources for children. Phone numbers and websites are below.

Oxfam: ww.oxfam.org.uk; 0870 333 2700

World Vision: www.worldvision.org.uk; 01908 841000

Tearfund: www.tearfund.org.uk; 0845 355 8355

Cafod: www.cafod.org.uk; 020 7730 7900

• Whom can you ask for help if you are frightened or worried? Talk about the five key people, or groups of people, that a child may trust: family they live with, friends of their own age, adults who work at their school, the police, yourself. Children can draw around their hands, then turn the fingers into drawings of five of the people. As a class, you could then talk about worrying or fearful situations and ask the children who could help them in each scenario. Could they help themselves? Would they need to talk to a parent? Would they need to talk to someone in school?

• Some other books that deal with fears and worries are *Tell me Something Happy before I go to sleep* by Joyce Dunbar and Debi Gliori (Doubleday) and *The Huge Bag of Worries* by Virginia Ironside (Hodder Wayland).

CIRCLE-TIME SUGGESTIONS

Fears are a difficult matter to discuss openly, but such discussion can be very comforting for children, helping them to realise that they are not alone in their worries. The main thrust of this circle time is not just that we share fears, but more importantly that we share our solutions and ways of handling fears. Using examples of your own childhood fears and how you overcame them, or accommodated them, will also help children to realise that their fears may not be with them forever.

Sentence stem

'Sometimes I am scared of/by . . .'

Extension

After this you might like to explore the issues a little more. Encourage the children to think of things that have helped them to conquer their fears. Did they manage this alone or did someone help them? If someone helped, what did they do that was helpful?

The Bear under the Stairs

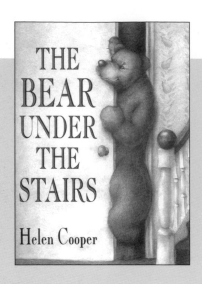

BOOK DETAILS

Author and illustrator: Helen Cooper

Publisher: Corgi Children's Books (1994)

ISBN: 0 552 52706 8

TOPICS

✓ *Worries and fears*

✓ *Sorting out problems*

✓ *Asking for help*

SUMMARY OF STORY

William is frightened of grizzly bears and of the cupboard under the stairs, where one day he thinks he sees a bear. William is worried about the bear and sneaks food to it to keep it happy. Eventually the food begins to smell and William's mum decides to do some cleaning. William admits to his fear and he and his mum tackle the problem head on.

THINGS TO THINK ABOUT

This story calls for parents to take their children's fears seriously.

As soon as William's mother discovers William's big fear – that William believes there is a big scary bear that lives under the stairs – his mother acts. She listens carefully to what William has to say, she gives him time, she takes his worries seriously, and she tackles the immediate problem and helps William with his fears in the longer term. At no point does she shout at him or tell him off about the food he has thrown under the stairs to placate the bear.

Although William's mother acts quickly when she discovers the problem, there were signs she missed earlier on in the story, in particular William's drawing of a truly terrifying bear. Sometimes in our busy lives we may find it difficult to spend time talking to children about their fears, especially if these fears appear to us to be ridiculous.

In a book with a similar theme, *Not now, Bernard* by David McKee (Red Fox Picture Books), the child tries to talk to his parents but they constantly say to him, 'Not now, Bernard.' Eventually Bernard is literally consumed by his fears. He really wanted someone to listen to him and talk with him about the scary monster he'd seen. We can all do that for our children.

We do need to acknowledge the child's fears. Saying 'Don't be silly, there's nothing to worry about,' will not help. We must certainly never say things like 'Don't be such a baby.' Taking children's worries seriously is explored in the 'Things to do or make' section.

THINGS TO DO OR MAKE

In the story William's mother could have used the chant 'We're Going on a Bear Hunt' with William as they set off to demystify the cupboard under the stairs. It is a great song for dealing with fears as it gets real, gets right and gets going (see page 59). In the song there is no avoiding the problems – when you come to the long grass, you can't go under it, you can't go round it, you can't go over it, you have to go through it – you have to face up to them. You could get hold of *We're Going on a Bear Hunt* by Michael Rosen and Helen Oxenbury (Walker Books Ltd) to explore this chant. You could say it together and go and check out a cupboard of your own.

You could also remember the line 'Get real, get right, get going', so that when your child is scared of something – the dentist, a new school term, whatever – you could say, 'Shall we go on a bear hunt and sort it out?'

THINGS TO TALK ABOUT

• Have you ever been frightened of anything, without good reason? Share this with your child.

• What frightens William?

• What does William think the bear might do to him?

• How does William try to cope with his fears?

• Why was this not a good idea? Talk with your child about practical reasons why William's plan did not work (for example, made the house smell). Also talk about emotional reasons why it was not a good idea, (you can't always placate people or things you are scared of).

• Look at the night-time picture of the house, when William dreams of all the things the bear might do when he is asleep. What can you see the bear doing? What is on the television? What does the bear like to play with in the attic? Where has one of the pancakes ended up in the kitchen?

• What does the bear use to light his way around the bedrooms? Why doesn't he just switch the light on?

• What put a stop to William's plan?

• Earlier in the book, William gave his mother a clue that he was thinking about something scary. What was the clue? (Hint – look at William's drawing.)

• How does William's mum help him to overcome his fears?

• Could William have overcome his fears on his own? When problems are too big for us to cope with on our own, it is OK to ask for help.

• Talk with your child about things that have worried them in the past and how those were resolved.

• Is there anything that is worrying your child at the moment? Ask what you can do to help with that worry and try to make a plan together.

However, there is a lot to be said for being a little bit creative with solutions to fears. Ideas we have known people have great success with include the following:

Scared of having bad dreams – find an old purse or small make-up bag. Collect symbols of things the child would like to dream about – for example, a picture of Granny, a small flower; you can even write words on a piece of paper and decorate it. Then at bedtime, look through the dream purse together and talk about the pleasant dreams the child is going to have. Place the dream purse under their pillow, give them a kiss, wish them sweet dreams and exit.

Afraid of the dark – stick glow-in-the-dark planets or fairies on the ceiling above your child's bed.

Afraid that Father Christmas won't come – ring, write/fax or email him.

Encourage your child to talk to adult friends and family members about what these people are frightened of. They could make a worries pact – 'I [child's name] promise to rescue [adult's name] from any spiders.' 'I [adult's name] promise to leave the landing light on until [child's name] is asleep.'

Lovely Old Roly

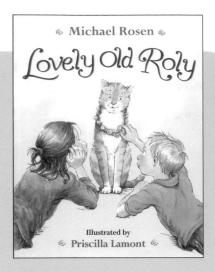

TOPICS

✓ *Being part of a family*

✓ *Bereavement and loss*

✓ *Valuing memories*

SUMMARY OF STORY

Roly the family cat grows old and dies. The children grieve for him and can't summon up the enthusiasm for their usual games. However, they discover that life has to go on, even though they feel sad at times. Eventually a new cat appears that they call Sausage. She is a nice cat and they like her. She comes to stay, most of the time. But Roly is with them all the time and keeps a place in their hearts.

FURTHER READING

Always and Forever by Alan Durant and Debi Gliori (Corgi Children's Books, 2004)

Michael Rosen's Sad Book by Michael Rosen and Quentin Blake (Walker Books Ltd, 2004)

Goodbye Mog by Judith Kerr (Picture Lions, 2003)

Badger's Parting Gifts by Susan Varley (Picture Lions, 1994)

TALKING POINTS

• How can the children tell that Roly is getting so old it's nearly time for him to die?

• Does he have a favourite blanket? What makes you think it is his favourite?

• What are some of the things the children do and say to show Roly that they love him?

• When Roly dies, what do the children do and say that show they want to remember him? Where do they put his body?

• Look at the pictures – what time of year is it when Roly died? How can you tell?

• Why don't the children want to play their usual games?

• What would the children be like if they forgot about Roly straightaway?

• Mum said they had to carry on with life even though they felt sad. What sort of things do they do?

• How do they feel while they are doing these things?

• After a while the children want a new pet. Why are they told it's too soon?

• What did they start to play again?

• How do you think you would play Danger Dog?

• Can you see the new cat looking at them? What does it look like?

• What time of year is it now?

• Look at the children's faces. Compare them to when they did not want to play games. Do they seem to be feeling better? How do you know?

• Eventually the new cat comes to play with them in their garden. What time of year is it now? How long has it been since Roly died?

• Look at Roly's grave. How has it changed?

• On the last page the children think Roly is 'with us all the time'. What do you think they mean? Look at the shape of the thought bubbles.

• Look at the children's eyes. Do you think they might be crying?

• Why would they be crying when they don't look sad?

• Look at their faces. Why do you think they don't look as sad as they were when Roly first died?

Author: Michael Rosen   Illustrator: Priscilla Lamont
Publisher: Frances Lincoln Ltd (2002)   ISBN: 0 7112 1489 1

CIRCLE-TIME SUGGESTIONS

Loss in its many forms is a sensitive subject to explore. You have to pick the right time. However, careful handling of the subject during circle time can be very helpful. As loss can cover many experiences, not just death, it can be good to cover it in different ways at different times. Other experiences that involve a sense of loss include moving house, moving school and divorce/separation. You could share some of your own experiences in such areas, depending on the age of the class, to show that it is possible to survive and grow after such events.

Sentence stem

You could use the sentence stem 'When I am sad I try . . .' to develop a bank of strategies for the children to draw on in times of need. You could record the ideas in written or pictorial form in a scrapbook and include it in your class library. This makes the book and what it includes part of everyday life and not something to be pulled out when tragedy strikes.

FOLLOW-UP ACTIVITIES

Death is never going to be an easy topic to discuss. In *Lovely Old Roly* we see the seasons pass. This is to help us see that as time passes the children slowly get over the death of Roly.

• **You could use pictures of people, animals and even plants and trees to talk to the children about how all living things are born, grow and die, some slowly and some quite speedily. It's not the dying that makes us sad; the sadness depends upon how much we loved that which has died.**

• **You can then talk about the things that are left behind by someone who has died: memories, things they taught us, things they made, ideas they had, their sayings, their favourite songs and stories they told us of their past.**

• **You could ask the children to bring in something (nothing valuable) that has been left behind by someone they loved – for example Grandma's scarf, Granddad's torch, a card or postcard they sent.**

ASSEMBLY IDEA

A colleague once did an assembly about death by talking about a raindrop. He started by describing an individual raindrop he watched trickling down the window until it plopped into a puddle in the playground. As the days passed and the sun came out, the puddle disappeared. One day it was there, and soon after it had gone. But, he explained, it had not just disappeared into nothingness. He told the children that it had evaporated. He then briefly explained how the water cycle works. He concluded by saying that after the raindrop had evaporated and returned to the sky, maybe it had fallen as a raindrop onto the sea and joined thousands of other drops of water in a mighty ocean.

He explained that water never leaves our planet, it goes around and around. He then talked about how, although things die, they do not disappear, leaving no trace. When people or much loved pets die, they stay alive in our memories. Maybe, like the raindrop, we cannot see them any more, but they are still somewhere – they are in our hearts and minds.

Lovely Old Roly

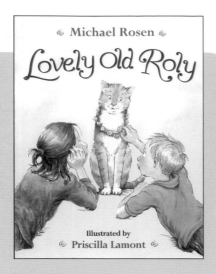

BOOK DETAILS

Author: Michael Rosen

Illustrator: Priscilla Lamont

Publisher: Frances Lincoln Ltd (2002)

ISBN: 0 7112 1489 1

TOPICS

✓ *Being part of a family*

✓ *Bereavement and loss*

✓ *Valuing memories*

SUMMARY OF STORY

Roly the family cat grows old and dies. The children grieve for him and can't summon up the enthusiasm for their usual games. However, they discover that life has to go on, even though they feel sad at times. Eventually a new cat appears that they call Sausage. She is a nice cat and they like her. She comes to stay, most of the time. But Roly is with them all the time and keeps a place in their hearts.

THINGS TO THINK ABOUT

There are times when reading this book would be too sad and painful. If, however, you take time to think about the subject of loss when it is not too distressing, you can prepare children for sadnesses that will inevitably come along.

The main hope of this conversation is to help children realise that we can move on from a place of great sadness. We can think about the importance of having lots of good memories of people or pets who have died to help this process. It will be helpful if you share with your child your happy family memories of those who have died.

THINGS TO TALK ABOUT

• **What kind things do the children do to make Roly's last days happy?**

• **What do the children say to show Roly that they love him?**

• **When Roly dies, what do Mum and Dad say so that the children know that they will always remember Roly?**

• **The children's mum says that Roly will 'always be in and around you somewhere'. What do you think she means?**

• **Where do they put Roly's body?**

• **Look at the pictures. What time of year is it when Roly dies?**

• **Why don't the children want to play their usual games?**

- Mum says they have to carry on, even though they feel sad. Do they do the sort of things we do together? Do they look very happy yet?

- When they start to play again, how long has it been since Old Roly died?

- What is the cat they see sitting on the fence like?

- How do you know that the children seem to be feeling happier?

- What time of year is it when the new cat comes to play in their garden?

- Why do they call the cat Sausage?

- Look at Roly's grave. How is it different from when it was dug? (At first pet graves in the garden are very painful, but as time passes you become less sad when you pass them. Eventually you can pass them with a happy memory of the dead pet. This helps you know that you will be able to survive something sad happening.)

- On the last page the children think Roly is 'with us all the time'. What do they mean?

- What do the shapes of the thought bubbles mean?

- Look at the children's faces. Are they as sad as they were when Roly died?

- Do you think they are remembering some of the things Roly used to do? What might they be thinking about?

THINGS TO DO OR MAKE

This could be a good day to dig out a few family albums and look at the photographs. Try to remember something about each person. For example: 'There's Uncle Bill, he used to build the best bonfire in the world when I was younger. And, look, there's his cat, Miss Miggs. She used to catch loads of mice.'

Try to help your child recognise things from the photographs and recall their own happy memories. For example: 'Look, who's that in the photograph? Yes, it's you and me on holiday when you were little. What are you holding? It's your old stuffed rabbit! Do you remember how you wouldn't go anywhere without Rabbit?'

If possible, look out a few things that you have had passed on to you by family members – vases, bits of jewellery, gloves, scarves, garden tools, whatever. Explain that when you look at these you remember the person to whom they used to belong. Once that would have made you sad, but now they bring happier memories.

Oscar Got the Blame

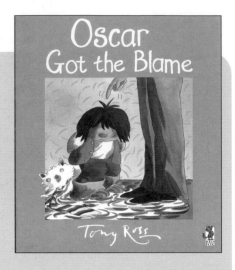

TOPICS

✓ *Imaginary friends*

✓ *Responsibility and blame*

✓ *Doing the right thing*

✓ *Being part of a family*

✓ *Misbehaviour*

✓ *Exploring reputation*

SUMMARY OF STORY

Oscar has an imaginary friend called Billy. Billy is always doing naughty things like putting frogs in Granny's slippers and dressing the dog in Dad's clothes. However, it is always Oscar who gets the blame, much to Billy's relief.

TALKING POINTS

- Who left the mud round the house? Are there any clues in the picture that help us answer this question?

- Why do you think the taps were left on in the bathroom?

- Why do you think Oscar offers Billy his dinner?

- Is Billy really there, or is he just in Oscar's imagination? What clues does the author offer us?

- Would you like to tell us about an imaginary friend you have had?

- Why do you think someone might have an imaginary friend?

- How is an imaginary friend better than a real friend? How are they not as good?

- What could Oscar have done differently after each event? What can we do if we have made a mess or a mistake? Talk about positive and negative options.

- Look at the picture of Dad's face after Oscar dressed the dog up. What words describe how he is feeling? How has his face changed to show his feelings?

- Compare the picture of Oscar on the first page with the picture of Billy near the end of the book. Are there any clues in the pictures to tell us whether Billy is real or just inside Oscar?

- Do we all have a Billy inside us? Do we also have a voice inside reminding us of the right thing to do?

- How can we make sure we listen to the right voice and ignore Billy?

MOTION FOR DEBATE

'This class believes that anger is a bad thing.'

Hold this debate before doing any of the additional activities. Children often think that anger is always unacceptable. The activities will help them to understand that everyone feels anger sometimes and sometimes rightly so. It is what we do with our anger that matters. Running this debate before the activities will encourage the children to think for themselves about situations when well-managed anger might be understandable or even a force for good.

Author and illustrator: Tony Ross
Publisher: Red Fox Picture Books (1995) ISBN 0 09 957280 X

FOLLOW-UP ACTIVITIES

• Take photographs of children smiling (being themselves) and photographs of them scowling (being the 'Billy inside'). Stick the pairs back to back. Use them in circle time and at other times to help children discuss taking responsibility for their own actions. You could ask them to show you themselves or the Billy inside, depending on the scene you outline. If it is a Billy scene, you could explore ways to put the situation right.

• Draw an imaginary good friend – the person who would remind you of the right thing to do. These drawings could be part of a display with target reminders, phrased in positive terms – for example: 'John, remember to have good break times', 'Shola, remember to share the play equipment.'

• The good, the bad and the ugly. Brainstorm with the class how people react when angry, covering a flipchart with suggestions. Type up the children's suggestions. In groups, give the children copies of the suggestions on strips of paper and a piece of A3 divided into three columns labelled *The good, The bad, The ugly*. Ask them to discuss in their groups whether each angry reaction is 'good' (i.e. allowing them to express their anger in a safe and acceptable way), 'bad' (i.e. less than ideal, but not the worst possible) or 'ugly' (i.e. something that is completely unacceptable). Stick the strips down in the appropriate columns, then discuss as a class. The most interesting discussions will be about the grey area of the 'bad' reactions. Everybody feels anger sometimes. In an ideal world we would all be able to handle our anger with only 'good' reactions. However, sometimes anger gets the better of us. This is particularly true of children, who are learning to manage their emotions. Discussing the range of possible angry reactions will allow them to make progress, even if that is from 'ugly' to 'bad' initially. We are not advocating behaviour that falls in the 'bad' column, just helping children to recognise that there is a spectrum of behaviour and improvement is possible. It is important to understand that children who have difficulties with their behaviour cannot change their reactions from 'ugly' to 'good' overnight. An improvement on 'bad' should be recognised, whilst never losing sight of the goal of 'good'. Use the 'good' reactions to make a class poster for everyone to refer to. Keep the good, bad and ugly group sheets as a resource for future discussions.

• Adult anger management. Activity for older children. Use the Internet to find out about organisations and people that help adults to manage anger and angry situations (e.g. Amnesty International [www.amnesty.org], ACAS [www.acas.co.uk], Fairtrade Foundation [www.fairtrade.org.uk]).

CIRCLE-TIME SUGGESTIONS

Circle Time is a good opportunity to explore taking responsibility for our actions. After doing the activity 'The good, the bad and the ugly', you might like to have a circle time using the sentence stem:

'Next time I feel like Billy I will try to . . .'.

Children can refer to the group sheets for the activity to choose an angry reaction that is an improvement on the way they have reacted in the recent past. For some this might mean choosing a 'bad' reaction, but that may be a huge improvement on the 'ugly' reaction that they normally display.

Oscar Got the Blame

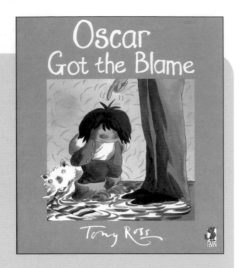

BOOK DETAILS

Author and illustrator: Tony Ross

Publisher: Red Fox Picture Books (1995)

ISBN: 0 09 957280 X

TOPICS

✓ *Imaginary friends*

✓ *Responsibility and blame*

✓ *Doing the right thing*

✓ *Being part of a family*

✓ *Misbehaviour*

✓ *Exploring reputation*

SUMMARY OF STORY

Oscar has an imaginary friend called Billy. Billy is always doing naughty things like putting frogs in Granny's slippers and dressing the dog in Dad's clothes. However, it is always Oscar who gets the blame, much to Billy's relief.

THINGS TO TALK ABOUT

- Is Billy real or not? Why do you think this? What clues do the illustrations offer?

- Do we all have a Billy inside? If so, how can we try to look after him so that he doesn't get us into trouble?

- If you had an imaginary friend as a child, tell your child about them before asking them if they have an imaginary friend.

- Look through the book at all the grown-ups. Look at their faces. Are they kind to Oscar? What makes you say that?

- Do any of the grown-ups ever play with Oscar?

- Why do you think Oscar does the things in the book? Is he trying to be helpful? Is he bored?

- Do the grown-ups talk to Oscar, or do they just tell him off?

- What could the grown-ups have done to occupy Oscar?

- What is wrong with the breakfast that Oscar makes? What would be a good breakfast?

- Oscar likes doing messy things. Look through the book for all the messy things he does. What messy things do your family enjoy doing?

- What should you do if you make a mess or a mistake at home? Share some times when each of you made a mess. How did you make things better?

THINGS TO DO OR MAKE

When Oscar tried to make breakfast on his own, it went horribly wrong, but making breakfast together can be fun. Agree what will be on the menu and choose a Saturday or Sunday when you can enjoy making and eating it together. You could each take a role for one part of the breakfast – Chief Bread Toaster, Expert Toast Butterer and Top Jam Spreader.

Look at the endpapers, the front and back inside covers of the book. Some editions of this book have handprints all over them. Making your own handprints using children's paint can be great fun. Start with a clean piece of paper and make a family handprint picture. Explore the different shapes you can make with your palm, your fist and your fingers. Who has the biggest handprint in the family? Who has the smallest? Work together to clean up any mess afterwards.

Look through the book at the different angry responses the adults display. Some of these are pretty violent – but sometimes little things can really wind us up. Have a family discussion about acceptable and unacceptable ways to show anger. You might also take the opportunity to try to sort out some frequent sources of irritation – for example: Mum might be cross that there are always wet towels on the floor and shoes in the hall, children might be cross that they are told to stop activities without any warning.

Look at the page where Oscar won't eat his dinner. Talk with your child about how Oscar looks when he has to eat it. Together, use magazines to make a collage of food that your child likes. You might also find pictures of new foods that your child would like to try. If you can't find printed pictures of a new food, your child could draw it.

Go for a wander around the fruit and vegetable aisles of a supermarket and see what strange new fruit and vegetables you could all try as a family. Look up some simple recipes that you can cook together. You might even compile your own cookery scrapbook filled with your child's favourite recipes.

On the Way Home

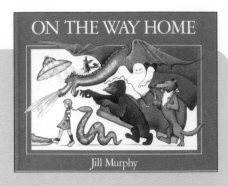

ON THE WAY HOME

Jill Murphy

TOPICS

✓ *Responsibility and blame*

✓ *Being honest*

✓ *Using our imagination*

✓ *Exploring reputation*

SUMMARY OF STORY

Claire is walking home to show her mum the cut on her knee. On the way she meets lots of her friends. Each time she meets a friend, she makes up a different elaborate story to explain how she got her bad knee. She tells the truth when she gets back home. Mum comforts her and gives her the biggest plaster in the packet to cover the cut.

TALKING POINTS

• Look at the first page. Do we know why Claire has a cut on her knee? What could have happened to her?

• When Claire meets each of her friends, who speaks first?

• What do you notice about what Claire says each time she meets a friend?

• Why do you think she wants people to notice her bad knee?

• What sort of stories does Claire tell?

• Do you recognise any of the characters in her stories? Where do you know them from?

• Is Claire a good storyteller? Pick out the words that make her stories exciting to hear.

• How does Claire escape each dangerous situation?

• How do her friends react to her stories? Look at their faces and what they say in each case. Do you think they believe her? Would you believe her?

• Why do you think there aren't any children in the pictures of the stories that Claire tells her friends?

• Why do you think Claire needed to make up the stories?

• Why wasn't she happy with the truth? Was the truth rather boring or embarrassing? Or was it for some other reason?

• Why did she make up a different story each time? Do you think she simply enjoys being imaginative and creative?

• What do you think her favourite subject is at school?

• How do you think telling the stories makes Claire feel?

• Why does Claire tell her mother the truth at the end of the story?

• Why do you think Claire wanted the biggest plaster in the whole box?

MOTION FOR DEBATE

'This class believes that friends should tell the truth to each other at all times.'

This can be an entertaining discussion that leads to thoughtful comments.

Author and illustrator: Jill Murphy
Publisher: Macmillan Children's Books (1982)   ISBN: 0 333 37572 6

CIRCLE-TIME SUGGESTIONS

You could use a circle time to explore the joys of storytelling in the right context. Begin with any interesting sentence. You could try:

'The door creaked open slowly.'

'From the window of the spaceship, she looked out onto a strange, new planet.'

'"You're not going out and that's final!" said Mum.'

Any sentence will do really. The children can add a sentence each as you go round the circle and see where the story takes them.

If you were feeling really inventive, you could start with the final sentence of a story and get the children to tell the story round the circle from the end to the beginning.

FOLLOW-UP ACTIVITIES

• Through a class discussion, think of several emergencies similar to those told by Claire, such as being chased by a lion, cornered by a troll, lost in a dark wood, or pursued by a pack of wolves. How would you escape from each situation? The children could write, tell or act out their stories. Encourage them to invent the most imaginative story and ingenious escape.

• You could take some of the stories you generated in the circle time and develop them into small plays or tableaux to share in assemblies or to show to another class. If it is a younger class, there is scope for lots of good discussion on making the work suitable for a particular audience.

ASSEMBLY IDEA

Either this book, or the stories that the children write, would be great acted out in an assembly. You could then have a question-and-answer session with the whole school about the issues from the story, exploring the delights of storytelling but also pointing out when it is important to tell the truth. Remind the children that Claire was only able to be helped and comforted when she told her mum the truth.

On the Way Home

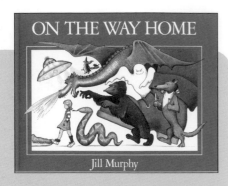

ON THE WAY HOME

Jill Murphy

BOOK DETAILS

Author and illustrator: Jill Murphy

Publisher: Macmillan Children's Books (1982)

ISBN: 0 333 37572 6

TOPICS

✓ *Responsibility and blame*

✓ *Being honest*

✓ *Using our imagination*

✓ *Exploring reputation*

SUMMARY OF STORY

Claire is walking home to show her mum the cut on her knee. On the way she meets lots of her friends. Each time she meets a friend, she makes up a different elaborate story to explain how she got her bad knee. She tells the truth when she gets back home. Mum comforts her and gives her the biggest plaster in the packet to cover the cut.

THINGS TO THINK ABOUT

As parents, we can sometimes get really worried about our children telling lies. Lots of children make up stories for many different reasons. It might be because the reality is too painful, or too embarrassing, or too dull.

We all need to feel significant, competent and powerful in our own lives. When these feelings are compromised, we may choose to borrow strength in different ways. Telling stories is just one of the ways this can be done. Think of a time when you have felt hurt, embarrassed or stupid and you doctored the truth in order to make yourself feel better.

In the questions below there are some that explore when telling the truth is important. This is not to negate the joy and fun of storytelling, but to help you and your child to look at those areas of life where the truth is paramount. This gives you an opportunity to talk to your child in a non-confrontational way about incidents where they could have been more truthful than they were, and the problems that were created because of that.

THINGS TO TALK ABOUT

• **How do you think Claire cut her knee?**

• **On the way home, why does Claire want people to look at her bad knee?**

• **Does Claire tell good stories? What makes them good? (Look at the words she uses to describe what happened to her.)**

• **What other stories do you know that include some of the characters that Claire mentions?**

• **How does Claire escape each dangerous situation that she tells her friends about?**

• **Do you think her friends believe Claire's stories? (Look at their expressions and the words they use.)**

• **Did you find any of the stories more believable than others? Which ones did you think were more believable and why?**

• **Why did Claire need to make up the stories? Why wasn't she happy with the truth? Was the truth rather boring or embarrassing?**

• **Was Claire being naughty?**

• **How did telling the stories make Claire feel?**

• **What is the big difference between a story and the truth?**

• **Why does Claire tell her mother the truth? Are there some people you should always tell the truth to? Why is that?**

THINGS TO DO OR MAKE

With older children, you could read all or parts of *The Eighteenth Emergency* by Betsy Byars (Red Fox, 2000). In this story, Benjie and his friend Ezzie devise solutions for seventeen emergencies, but they cannot decide on a solution for the eighteenth, when Benjie gets on the wrong side of the school bully, Marv Hammerman. This story explores some issues to do with growing up, being bullied and facing fears.

The Tiger who Came to Tea by Judith Kerr (Collins Picture Book, 1992) is a good book for looking at the creative element of storytelling with younger children.

Play wild stories. Give your child a scenario and ask them to invent a wild story. Then they give you a scenario and you have to invent a wild story. Here is an example:

You: Why haven't you tidied your room?

Child: Because when I went upstairs I found a grumpy-looking dwarf sitting on my bed. He was on a quest to find dragon's treasure but said he was very tired. So he had climbed through my open window and was trying to sleep on my bed. I didn't want to make him any more grumpy, and so I crept out quietly and came downstairs. And that's why I didn't tidy my room.

You: That's a wild story! Now what's the truth?

Child: I wanted to watch *The Simpsons* instead.

Next, your child could give you a starting question for a wild story.

The scenarios that you use could be real-life incidents or imaginary ones. You can play this game for ages, taking turns to tell a wild story. The aim of the game is to develop imagination, but not lose sight of the difference between truth and fiction.

The True Story of the 3 Little Pigs!

TOPICS

✓ *Responsibility and blame*

✓ *Being honest*

✓ *Making choices*

✓ *Exploring reputation*

SUMMARY OF STORY

The wolf, speaking from his prison cell, tells his side of the traditional story of the Three Little Pigs and tries to convince us that he was not responsible for what befell the animals. The wolf's word is not necessarily to be entirely trusted, though.

TALKING POINTS

• How would you describe the wolf's character in his version of the story? How would you describe the pigs?

• How are these descriptions different from those in the traditional story?

• Why does the wolf want us to believe it was not his fault?

• Do you believe the wolf's story? Give reasons for your choice.

• Does the wolf deserve his reputation? He blames it on the news reporters. Can you think of any real-life news stories that have created or destroyed someone's reputation?

• Should the wolf be blamed for eating the pigs?

• Does it make a difference if the pigs died accidentally before he ate them or not?

• Is it fair that wolves are described as big and bad because they 'eat cute little animals like bunnies and sheep and pigs'?

• Do you have a reputation? What do you think your reputation is based on?

• Do other people know the real you, as opposed to the you they think they know?

• What could you do to show people what you are really like?

• Have you ever made up a story to cover up a mistake?

• What was the outcome?

• How did you feel about that afterwards?

• Why is it sometimes hard to accept responsibility for our actions?

• In what ways could you try to be more responsible?

MOTION FOR DEBATE

'This class believes that one difference between us and animals is that, unlike animals, we can always choose how to behave.'

Author: Jon Scieszka   Illustrator: Lane Smith
Publisher: Puffin Books (1991)   ISBN: 0 14 054056 3

FOLLOW-UP ACTIVITIES

Hold a hot-air balloon debate. Write on a balloon drawn on a flipchart the names of storybook villains. The children pick a villain and try to persuade the rest of the class that they should be allowed to stay in the balloon. For example:

'The troll had been asleep under his bridge, and the trip trapping had woken him up and put him in a grumpy mood. His bridge was old and he was worried that the billy goats gruff would damage it. He would never have eaten them. He just wanted to look after his bridge.'

CIRCLE-TIME SUGGESTIONS

This is a good way to find out hidden and surprising secrets about each other. using this sentence stem:

'Something you don't know about me is . . .'

The next sentence stem can lead on to a discussion about the nature of responsibility and how it is better to take it than to avoid it.

'When I realise I have done something wrong, my response is to . . .'

Extension

Explore the issues a little. Encourage the children to think of more appropriate ways to react in the situations they mention.

FOLLOW-UP ACTIVITIES

The real me. Each child makes a poster with a photograph of themselves in the centre of it. It should be fixed with a hinge of sticky tape so that it can be raised. Each child writes or draws things everyone knows about them around their photograph. Underneath the photograph they write or draw things that people don't know about them. These could be presented on a display board or in a scrapbook so that the children have easy access to them.

Re-write or re-tell a different familiar story from another point of view. For example, how would the giant tell the story of Jack and the Beanstalk? Record this on tape or CD for younger children who know the original story.

Role-play scenarios in which a mistake has been made. These could be familiar dilemmas in school, such as a joke that backfired with someone being hurt or picking up something that is not yours.

How could the situation be resolved by the main character taking responsibility immediately?

What would happen if a story were told to cover up the mistake instead?

- In which sort of situations is telling a story OK?

- What sort of situations are there in which telling a story is not OK and may make things worse?

- There is a poster on page 108 that needs to be copied with the 'For home' materials for this book.

The True Story of the 3 Little Pigs!

BOOK DETAILS

Author: Jon Scieszka

Illustrator: Lane Smith

Publisher: Puffin Books (1991)

ISBN: 0 14 054056 3

TOPICS

✓ *Responsibility and blame*

✓ *Being honest*

✓ *Making choices*

✓ *Exploring reputation*

SUMMARY OF STORY

The wolf, speaking from his prison cell, tells his side of the traditional story of the Three Little Pigs and tries to convince us that he was not responsible for what befell the animals. The wolf's word is not necessarily to be entirely trusted, though.

THINGS TO THINK ABOUT

Have you ever made up a story to cover up a mistake? It's good to bring to mind the feelings associated with doing this before you talk with your child about this subject. You could tell your child about the incident, so that they know that you have been there too and know what it feels like.

THINGS TO TALK ABOUT

• Do you think the wolf is lying? Give reasons for your choice.

• What makes you think that he might not be telling the whole truth?

• Should the wolf be blamed for eating the pigs or is he just doing what wolves do?

• He finds the pigs as tempting as a cheeseburger. What do you find tempting?

• What might tempt you into trouble?

• What does the wolf mean when he says 'Wolf's honour'?

• How much do you think the news reporters are to blame for the wolf's reputation? Do you think they treated him fairly? If not, how could they have acted differently?

• Look at the last picture. How do you know that the wolf has been in prison for quite a while?

• Have you ever covered up a mistake by telling a story? What happened? (Your child might need a reminder of a recent incident. Make sure you talk about it in a positive light, though.)

• What could you have done instead?

• Why is it hard to tell the truth sometimes?

• Do you have a reputation for being responsible at school?

• What responsibilities do you have at home?

THINGS TO DO OR MAKE

Play Mad Excuses. Take turns to make up crazy reasons for things you should have done – for example, I couldn't lay the table because a metal virus infected all the knives and forks and they ran away and hid under the freezer.

Get Real, Get Right, Get Going! is a good formula to face up to responsibilities. You have to do this:

Face up to things – Get Real

Choose to get help from someone sensible and kind – Get Right

Sort things out – Get Going!

For example:

Get Real I have to be more responsible for my belongings.

Get Right Mum and I talked and agreed a plan.

Get Going! I will tidy my room once a week and as long as things are cared for, Mum will try not to nag me in between.

How could the wolf have acted on this advice? How would the story have changed?

Remember: Get Real   Get Right   Get Going!

Use the copy of the poster supplied with these materials next time there is a problem at home. You can then plan how to recognise a problem, discuss it with your child and come up with an agreed plan that works for all.

The Princess Knight

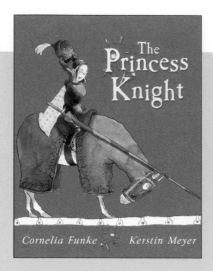

The
Princess
Knight

Cornelia Funke · Kerstin Meyer

TOPICS

✓ *Living with siblings*

✓ *Understanding differences*

✓ *Making choices*

✓ *Being a hero*

SUMMARY OF STORY

When Princess Violetta is born, her mother dies. The king decides to bring up his daughter in the same way as he brought up his sons, to be a knight. Princess Violetta wants to be a more skilful knight than her three brothers, who simply tease her for being small and weak. So Violetta sneaks out at night and secretly practises to become a better knight than they are. Her father decides to have a tournament and to allow the winner to marry Violetta. Violetta enters the tournament in disguise and wins it, defeating all the other knights who enter, owing to her nimbleness and speed. Many years later, Violetta marries the rose gardener's son, who kept watch for her when she secretly trained at night.

TALKING POINTS

- Violetta's father is called King Wilfred the Worthy. What does it mean to be worthy? (You might need the help of a dictionary for this question.)

- Do you think he lives up to his name?

- What did Violetta's brothers learn from their father?

- What was the most important thing they learned, in the eyes of the king?

- Do you agree that giving orders was the most important? What else do you think they should have learned as well, or instead of this?

- Why do you think that no one would tell the king how to raise his daughter?

- The king made a decision to teach Violetta the same things as he taught his sons. Do you think that was a good idea?

- How do you think Violetta felt during her lessons? Can you tell us about a time when you have felt the same?

- Did Violetta's brothers make things better or worse? How could they have acted differently?

- What does Emma think Violetta should learn to do instead?

- What do you think of her suggestions?

- What does Emma say are Violetta's strengths?

- Compare Violetta's approach to the skills of riding and fighting to her brothers' approach. Why do you think Violetta is a better knight?

- Why do you think that the king decides to hold a tournament and find a husband for Violetta?

- Does this fit with his decision to treat her in the same way as his sons?

- What does Violetta's brother think is the reason she is crying?

- Why do you think she is crying?

- What do the names of the knights who come to the tournament tell you about their characters?

- If Violetta were allowed to joust under her own name, what title do you think she should have? Lady Violetta the . . . ?

- What does Violetta win? Is it just the horse the king gives her later, or something more?

- Why do you think Violetta chose to marry the rose gardener's son?

Author: Cornelia Funke   Illustrator: Kerstin Meyer
Publisher: The Chicken House (2001)   ISBN: 1 904442 14 5

MOTION FOR DEBATE

'This class believes that the world would be a better place if girls were in charge.'

This debate is not intended to be anti-boys. It should allow you to discuss the strengths of boys and girls, things they have in common and the way they complement each other. It needs careful handling to ensure that the boys feel affirmed.

FOLLOW-UP ACTIVITIES

Look at famous people who are successful and respected without being aggressive. Here are examples:

• **Frank Lampard behaves well on the pitch while others are violent, and Frank Lampard is still respected.**

• **Jamie Oliver tries to improve children's health, and is not only interested in his own celebrity.**

• **Natasha Bedingfield lives a healthy life, while some other pop singers show off about the bad lifestyle they have.**

Make a display of heroes. Try to find people who are both cool and good. You could display photographs, magazine clippings and newspaper articles. Add captions that explain why they are included. This will help the children to look at aspects of behaviour and responsibility in role models.

CIRCLE-TIME SUGGESTIONS

Talk about things that children have made an effort at practising, in or out of school. For example, they might talk about how they have practised a musical instrument, a football skill, handwriting, spelling, keeping their temper or swimming. Use the sentence stem:

'I have spent time practising . . .'.

Have a circle time discussion which asks the children to reflect on the improvements they have made. Encourage them to realise that these improvements have been made because they persevered.

ASSEMBLY IDEA

Have a parade of heroes. Allow some children to dress up as their chosen hero and tell the rest of the school about them. Then introduce the idea of the hero inside yourself (while listening to 'Search for the Hero' by M People from the Ultimate Collection). Explore what could be done in school that would make you heroes. You could use the list of ideas as part of an action plan to update and review on a termly basis. This could include sections on helping others in the school, in the community, and round the world. Make each term's aims visible for the children – displays, assemblies and newsletters all help. Regular updates will keep the aims fresh and give a sense of progress. Arrange a celebration at the end of term to enjoy the sense of achievement and change.

The Princess Knight

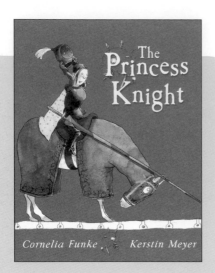

BOOK DETAILS

Author: Cornelia Funke

Illustrator: Kerstin Meyer

Publisher: The Chicken House (2001)

ISBN: 1 904442 14 5

TOPICS

✓ *Living with siblings*

✓ *Understanding differences*

✓ *Making choices*

✓ *Being a hero*

SUMMARY OF STORY

When Princess Violetta is born, her mother dies. The king decides to bring up his daughter in the same way as he brought up his sons, to be a knight. Princess Violetta wants to be a more skilful knight than her three brothers, who simply tease her for being small and weak. So Violetta sneaks out at night and secretly practises to become a better knight than they are. Her father decides to have a tournament and to allow the winner to marry Violetta. Violetta enters the tournament in disguise and wins it, defeating all the other knights who enter, owing to her nimbleness and speed. Many years later, Violetta marries the rose gardener's son, who kept watch for her when she secretly trained at night.

THINGS TO THINK ABOUT

This book has some stereotypes in it. Many of the boys are portrayed as stupid and violent. Violetta and Emma are calm and clever. Unfortunately, there seem to be many children's books that reinforce these stereotypes. However, this doesn't mean that the book is all bad. In fact, it offers the opportunity to talk with your child about the way boys and girls are portrayed in books and whether it is always fair. *Bill's New Frock* by Anne Fine (Egmont Books, 2002) is a good story to use to explore this issue further.

A good and important message from *The Princess Knight*, for boys and girls, is that might does not always equal right. Often the best way to get something done is to use tact and gentleness rather than force and fury.

As adults, we can use more of Violetta's skills (rather than those of her brothers) to explain to our children what is happening and why.

THINGS TO TALK ABOUT

- **How do the king's sons behave to the members of the royal household?**

- **What sort of things do they learn when they are growing up?**

- **Are there better things that they could be learning?**

- **Why does the king decide to teach Violetta the same things as her brothers?**

- **Do you think he is right to do this?**

- **How do you think Violetta felt during her lessons? Has there ever been a time when you have felt the same?**

- **Did Violetta's brothers make things better or worse? Do you and your siblings sometimes tease each other as they teased Violetta?**

- What else could Violetta's brothers have done, rather than teasing her and being unkind?

- In the book, Violetta fights her brothers and the other knights in order to be respected. She wins because she is kind (she doesn't use spurs on the horse), skilful (she is nimble and quick) and calm (she doesn't shout). Are these good skills to use to get what we want in life?

- How could you make use of them?

- Violetta has a rose on her shield. Why do you think she chose this?

- What would you have on your shield to represent you if you were a knight?

- Violetta doesn't want to be given a husband, she wants to choose one. How does she change the king's mind? (First she shouts, but this only gets her locked up in the castle. Then she uses her skills to devise a plan and show the king that she is worthy of making her own choice.)

- What else could the king have done, instead of telling Violetta what was going to happen to her?

- Could he have talked to her? Could he have listened to her? What might he have learned?

- Violetta went 'far, far away' for a year and a day after the tournament. Where do you think she went? What do you think she did?

- Violetta found a way out of her situation, but sometimes we have to accept the inevitability of certain changes, even when we might not like them. If a change is going to happen anyway, what can we do to cope with it better?

THINGS TO DO OR MAKE

Help your child to draw their shield. You could do this with coloured pencils or felt pens on a sheet of paper. However, if you want to try a bigger project you could use whatever materials you can get hold of easily – feathers, shells, foil, paint. Mount the shield on some card – the back of a cereal box will be fine.

If you are facing a family or individual change, look back through your family photograph albums and find pictures that remind you of changes in the past that turned out well.

Talk about how you all coped with the change – for example, looking at a photograph of a house you used to live in, remember how you liked living there and were sad to leave, but also talk about how much you like the next house.

Think about some of the things you did that made the change easier to manage. Now think about how you are going to behave while handling the new change you are facing.

Where the Wild Things Are

WHERE THE WILD THINGS ARE

STORY AND PICTURES BY MAURICE SENDAK

TOPICS

✓ *Friendship and belonging*

✓ *Doing the right thing*

✓ *Being part of a family*

✓ *Making choices*

✓ *Transfer to a new school*

✓ *Forgiveness*

✓ *Misbehaviour*

✓ *Exploring reputation*

SUMMARY OF STORY

One night, Max puts on his wolf suit and makes mischief, so his mother sends him to bed without any supper. In Max's room, a forest starts to grow and he goes on a magical journey across an ocean to the place where the wild things are. Max tames the wild things and they make him their king. Max has a great celebration with the wild things, but he soon misses home. He returns to his room, much to the wild things' disappointment, to find his supper there waiting for him.

TALKING POINTS

• What kinds of mischief does Max make?

• How does Max's wolf suit affect his behaviour?

• What reputation do wolves have? How might Max's behaviour have been different if he had dressed as another animal – for example, a cat, elephant, lion or snake?

• What mischief might he have made then?

• Plot Max's feelings through the book. How does he feel when:

> *he makes mischief;*   *he is sent to his room;*   *the forest grows;*
>
> *he sees the first monsters;*   *he is made king;*   *he returns home?*

• Why do you think the wild things think Max is the wildest thing of all?

• Think of some reasons why Max should stay with the wild things. Think of some reasons why he should return home. Perhaps you could debate what he should do.

• Max is torn between being wild with his new friends and going home. Have you ever felt like Max?

• Why do you think Max sent the wild things to bed without any supper?

• The smell of supper reminds Max of home. What reminds you of home?

Additional talking points for older children

• There are times, such as moving to a new school or being in the top year, when we can be tempted to become a wild thing. We might even go so far as to become king of the wild things. Sometimes we feel as if we have gone so far from being good, that nobody would ever let us be our good selves again. How might remembering Max help you?

• What did Max say at the end of the wild rumpus? Could we say 'I want to stop'?

• What do the wild things say to Max when he tries to leave? (First they plead with him to stay, and then they threaten him.) Has that kind of thing happened to you? Why does this happen?

• What sort of names are sometimes used by others when someone decides they want to change their behaviour?

• Are you sometimes worried that people will say 'We won't forgive you'? Do you get frightened that if you said you were sorry, people would still punish you or be cross?

• In fact, most people are really pleased when somebody who has been a bit wild decides to sail back home to their good self.

• Just as Max's supper was still hot, you can always return to your good self. When people see that you are serious about not being a wild thing any more, they will forgive you.

Author and illustrator: Maurice Sendak
Publisher: Red Fox Picture Books (2000)   ISBN: 0 09 940839 2

CIRCLE-TIME SUGGESTIONS

Talk about times when you have been tempted to be big and bad. What helped / could have helped you to make the right choice? Use the sentence stem below to explore both aspects of this suggestion:

'I feel tempted to be a wild thing when . . . Instead I could . . .'

Additional sentence stems for older children

Talk about when you have wanted to be forgiven, but nobody seems to want to forgive you.

'One of the problems with saying sorry is . . .'

'Sometimes I find it difficult to accept apologies when/if/because . . .'

FOLLOW-UP ACTIVITIES

Set the children some dilemmas – for example, 'Your friend wants you to hang out with them, but you have chores to do.' Ask them to role-play or discuss all the possible outcomes of this dilemma and identify the best solution or compromise.

Additional activity for older children

What was the route that Max took to leave the island where he was king of the wild things? (First he had to decide that he wanted to stop. Then he had to decide what he was going to do instead. It took him some time to make the return journey, but when he got back, he was forgiven.)

This is an opportunity to use the Get Real, Get Right, Get Going! poster on page 108. How did Max follow that advice? Put the poster up so you can plot the story against it.

Spend some time thinking about common dilemmas children face at home and how the Get Real, Get Right, Get Going! poster could help them. For example:

Get Real How can I play with my younger brother/sister and enjoy some time on my own?

Get Right I could talk it through with Mum/Dad to see if we can find a way that works for all of us.

Get Going! I will play with my brother/sister before lunch. After lunch, I can do my own thing and Mum/Dad will take over playing with my brother/sister.

Where the Wild Things Are

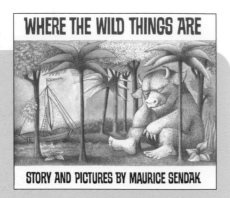

BOOK DETAILS

*Author and illustrator:
Maurice Sendak*

*Publisher: Red Fox Picture
Books (2000)*

ISBN: 0 09 940839 2

TOPICS

✓ *Friendship and belonging*

✓ *Doing the right thing*

✓ *Being part of a family*

✓ *Making choices*

✓ *Transfer to a new school*

✓ *Forgiveness*

✓ *Misbehaviour*

✓ *Exploring reputation*

SUMMARY OF STORY

One night, Max puts on his wolf suit and makes mischief, so his mother sends him to bed without any supper. In Max's room, a forest starts to grow and he goes on a magical journey across an ocean to the place where the wild things are. Max tames the wild things and they make him their king. Max has a great celebration with the wild things, but he soon misses home. He returns to his room, much to the wild things' disappointment, to find his supper there waiting for him.

THINGS TO THINK ABOUT

This is a book about unconditional love. Max's mother does not put up with Max's awful behaviour for a moment. When he behaves badly she still loves him, but sends him to his room. However, when he decides to change his behaviour and stop being a wild thing, she welcomes him back. His supper is there and it is still hot. Max's mother manages the difficult trick of enforcing the boundaries, while still offering him the security of her affection.

This book is also about how badly children can occasionally behave. Sometimes parents think that their child is the most dreadfully behaved child that ever was, but they are not. All children may behave really wildly at times. In this story Max not only wants to join the wild things, but becomes king of the wild things. However, he makes the choice to say 'Enough!' He decides to calm down and 'sail back home'.

The key is teaching our children that they are responsible for their own behaviour. It won't do just to say 'I'm angry because you made me!' That implies that somebody else is in charge of your behaviour. Children have to learn that they are in charge of themselves and always will be. When angry, how they manage that anger is their choice. We have to equip them with the knowledge that this choice exists and teach them some practical ways out of angry situations.

THINGS TO TALK ABOUT

• What does Max do that makes his mother unhappy?

• Do you sometimes lose your temper and sail away to a place where you are very cross inside yourself?

• What sort of place is it?

• Does Max cause the forest to grow in his bedroom?

• Do you sometimes get so cross that you are like a king of the wild things?

• What sort of things are you tempted to do when you are king of the wild things?

• What would your wild rumpus be like?

• Although Max has fun with the wild things, eventually he wants to go home. Do you sometimes feel sorry that you have been such a wild thing?

• Is it difficult to say sorry? Why is that, do you think?

• Do you think that people are sometimes worried that their family will say 'We won't forgive you'? Perhaps they get frightened that if they said they were sorry, their family will still be cross with them.

• What do you think Max had for his supper that smelled good?

• Just as Max's supper was still hot, you can always return to your good self. When people see that you are serious about not being a wild thing any more, they will forgive you.

THINGS TO DO OR MAKE

Everyone needs to let off steam sometimes. Have a wild rumpus! Put on a favourite piece of music and dance around together.

Have a look at the wild things in the book. Which one do you think is the scariest? All the wild things look as if they are made up of other animals. What animal parts can you recognise? Draw or make a collage of your own wild thing. Does any bit of it look like you?

Talk about little clues that everybody in the family gives when they are getting cross and becoming a wild thing – for example, maybe Mum goes pink in the face. What can we do to help someone cool down so they don't become a wild thing? You could make a list for each person and stick them to the fridge to serve as reminders when things get heated.

Work together to create a family wild thing using pencils, pens, paints, collage materials – whatever comes to hand. Use the book for ideas. It could have recognisable features of each family member to show that everyone has the potential to be a wild thing from time to time.

When managing a conversation with an angry child, the following structure can be useful:

1. Acknowledge that your child is unhappy – for example, 'I can see that you are really upset about this. Let's see if we can sort it out.'

2. Enquire about what has happened. Listen carefully.

3. Repeat back to them what they have said to you – for example, 'So what you are saying is . . .'

4. Encourage them to make suggestions about how they can resolve the situation – for example, 'You are a clever child, let's see if you can come up with some ideas. What do you think you could do?' This may involve some negotiation, but should result in a fair solution acceptable to all parties involved.

Always remember, when confronted with an angry situation, listen and act with kindness and patience.

Susan Laughs

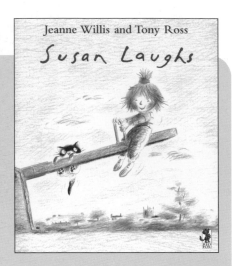

Jeanne Willis and Tony Ross
Susan Laughs

TOPICS

✓ *Friendship and belonging*

✓ *Making the most of every day*

✓ *Understanding differences*

✓ *Inclusion*

SUMMARY OF STORY

Susan is a little girl of about 6. She is a normal little girl who likes singing and playing with her friends. She is sometimes good and sometimes bad, sometimes happy and sometimes sad. In fact, she is much the same as every other little girl of 6, except that on the last page we see she is in a wheelchair. We realise this makes absolutely no difference to Susan being just like any other little girl, except that she needs a little help at times. Her family and friends seem to have got that covered.

TALKING POINTS

• You need to discuss how we have to face up to other people's difficulties. There is no point in pretending Susan is just like all of her friends. She isn't; she can't walk.

• We need to consider everyone's difficulties and yet find the ways we are alike and the things we can do together.

• Talk about what makes Susan who she is. It is the things that she likes and the things she doesn't like. It is the things she is good at and the things she is hopeless at. It is how well she gets on with her family and all the other people who love her. It is her sense of fun and her fears.

• Look through the story and find examples of each of these things. Spend some time relating Susan's experiences to those of children in the class.

> *Do they play a musical instrument?*

> *Do they like the roundabout at the park?*

> *What sort of dancing do they most enjoy?*

> *When do they feel shy?*

• Discuss how these things are what make us who we are. We are not defined by just one aspect of ourselves, especially not by a bit that doesn't work well. It is not Susan's legs that make Susan who she is, it's her personality, her talents and skills, the things she likes or doesn't like. It's also the people who love her who make her who she is.

• How do people in the story relate to Susan? Do they treat her exactly like a fully able-bodied person or do they make some allowances?

MOTION FOR DEBATE

'This class believes that opposites attract.'

This debate encourages the children to reflect on what makes a good friendship.

Author: Jeanne Willis   Illustrator: Tony Ross
Publisher: Red Fox Picture Books (2001)   ISBN: 0 09 940756 6

CIRCLE-TIME SUGGESTIONS

Play Positive Introductions. Put the children into pairs and ask them to find out something that their partner likes doing. After a few minutes, form a circle with each pair sitting next to each other. Allow each pair to introduce each other to the circle using the sentence stem: 'This is . . . and they like . . .'.

Sentence stem

Ask the children to think about activities they could do with Susan if she were in their class. 'If Susan were in our class we could . . .'. If the children make suggestions that are inappropriate, such as 'We could play skipping', stop them and discuss why that might not work. Then ask them to think of a way to make it work – for example, 'Susan could turn the rope and call out the skipping rhymes.'

FOLLOW-UP ACTIVITIES

If you have a digital camera available, make a large collage of photographs on a noticeboard of all of the class engaged in the same kind of activities as Susan in the book. Put labels near each of the photographs as in the book, saying who the person is and what they are doing. An example is 'Our class laughs.' There is no need to highlight anyone's difficulties. Try to ensure each child appears several times in different groups. Try to include all the adults who are involved with your class in the activity – teaching assistant(s), learning support assistant(s), lunchtime supervisor, school secretary, head teacher.

ASSEMBLY IDEA

Tell the children that you have received a letter from the government, explaining a new initiative. From now on, school will focus on the skills of dancing, singing and sport, rather than English, maths and science. Talk to them about how the timetable will have to change and how school reward systems will now recognise achievement in the new areas only. They must all work as hard as they can at dancing, singing and sport. There will be tests at the end of the week.

Then reveal to the children that the letter was not real, but ask them how it made them feel. Who was pleased about the change and thought they would do well in the new tests? Who was unhappy because they are successful in the traditional areas but not so good at dancing or singing? Explain that schools try to make everyone, whatever their talents, feel included. Ask the children to identify activities or systems at your school that help to do this – for example, a school reward system that recognises achievement in all areas, awards or competitions for non-SATs subjects.

Susan Laughs

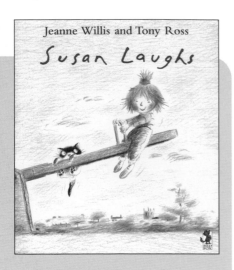

BOOK DETAILS

Author: Jeanne Willis

Illustrator: Tony Ross

Publisher: Red Fox Picture Books (2001)

ISBN: 0 09 940756 6

✓ *Friendship and belonging*

✓ *Making the most of every day*

✓ *Understanding differences*

✓ *Inclusion*

SUMMARY OF STORY

Susan is a little girl of about 6. She is a normal little girl who likes singing and playing with her friends. She is sometimes good and sometimes bad, sometimes happy and sometimes sad. In fact, she is much the same as every other little girl of 6, except that on the last page we see she is in a wheelchair. We realise this makes absolutely no difference to Susan being just like any other little girl, except that she needs a little help at times. Her family and friends seem to have got that covered.

TALKING POINTS

- Once you have got to the last page on the first reading, most children will be quite disconcerted. As you re-read the book, you will need to stop and look carefully to see that although on each page Susan is very busy, we never see her walk.

- Go through the book a third time, looking at each page and relating it to your child. For example: 'Susan is laughing at a television programme. She looks like you when you watch . . .', 'Oh, look at Susan and her friends singing. They have made a little band. Which song would you sing with your friends if you formed a band?'

- Go through the book in this way. Along the way, recall your child's happy memories, discuss their good friends and review their triumphs and tragedies.

- You can talk at the end about Susan's legs. They don't work, but that doesn't stop her having a happy life.

- What would make her life unhappy? (Children being frightened of her because she is in a wheelchair or leaving her out of things would definitely make her life sadder.)

- Talk to your child about the things that make us who we are. We are not defined by just one aspect of ourselves, especially not by a bit that doesn't work well. It is not Susan's legs that make Susan who she is, it's her personality, her talents and skills, the things she likes or doesn't like. It's also the people who love her who make her who she is.

- Think about any of your child's friends or family who may be different in some way. Think about all the things they like doing and that make them happy. Talk about ways in which they are just like your child, without ignoring the points of difference.

THINGS TO DO OR MAKE

Look around your garden or your child's bedroom or the local play area, thinking together about all of the things that your child could do with Susan if she came to play. If your child makes suggestions that are inappropriate, such as 'We could climb on the climbing frame', stop them and discuss why that wouldn't work. Then ask them to think of a way to make it work – for example, 'We could carry Susan to the top of the climbing frame, and we could sit on the seating area and have a picnic.'

This is one of those stories that you need to be able to remember when your child is just beginning to get to know a child who has a disability of one sort or another, or is noticeably different in some way. Help your child to remember Susan and encourage them to find out all of the things they may have in common with this potential new friend.

Friends' diagram. This is a way of appreciating how similarities and differences can make good friends. Show your child a photograph of you and a close friend. Talk about what you have in common and how those similarities have been good for your friendship (for example, both liking tennis). Then identify some differences that have contributed to your relationship (for example, living in different towns so you stay at each other's houses). Record these similarities and differences as a diagram, with a photograph of you by one list and one of your friend by the other. The children can complete their own diagrams in this way. Afterwards you could talk about some of the similarities and differences they have with their friend. This should help the children to realise that individual differences make life and friendships interesting.

Look What I've Got!

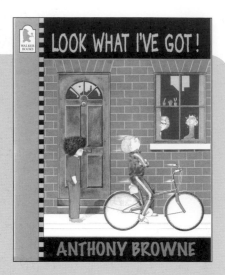

TOPICS

✓ *Making the most of every day*

✓ *Understanding differences*

✓ *Using our imagination*

✓ *Valuing special things*

✓ *Jealousy*

SUMMARY OF STORY

Jeremy always has new things – a bicycle, a pirate outfit, a bag of sweets – and he always boasts about them to Sam. But Sam doesn't seem bothered or jealous, and uses his imagination to see exciting things in the world around him that make his life far from dull.

TALKING POINTS

- This book can be seen from two perspectives: Sam's and Jeremy's. In many ways, they connect only occasionally. It is really important to read the book through once without interruption, because it is only at the end of the book that you will understand Sam's perspective.

- What do you think about Jeremy?

- What do you think about Sam?

- What do you think it would take for Jeremy to be a bit more thoughtful?

- On the double-page spread where Jeremy rides and crashes his bike (outside the house with the green front door), Sam doesn't seem very interested in Jeremy and his bicycle. What else do you think he might be looking at?

  What might Sam think of the old lady in the window? What does his imagination turn her into?

  What does the big strong man in the upstairs window remind Sam of?

  What does Sam think the letterbox might do to his hand? Or to letters?

  In the fanlight window of the door on the left-hand page, what is flying in the sky? Is it a bird? Is it a plane? Is it a flying saucer? (No, it's a flying cup!)

  How many differences are there between the two pages?

- Why doesn't Jeremy see any of these things?

- Look at other pages in the book in the same way, asking yourself 'What is Jeremy interested in?' and 'What unusual things does Sam see instead?'

- Jeremy's favourite phrase is 'Look what I've got!' Does Jeremy himself do much looking?

- Almost all the way through the book, Jeremy's eyes are closed. Find the two pages where he has his eyes wide open. What has to happen to make him open his eyes?

- Sam's eyes are open, as is his imagination. He sees small details and his imagination makes them interesting or humorous. Look at the last page of the book. Why doesn't Sam need to go to the zoo? What does he see in the woods?

- How many animals can you see on the last page? (We think there are fifteen.)

MOTION FOR DEBATE

'This class believes that you can't have fun without toys.'
This raises some interesting questions regarding imaginary games and role play that could have positive effects on school playtimes.

Author and illustrator: Anthony Browne
Publisher: Walker Books Ltd (1996) ISBN: 0 7445 4372 X

CIRCLE-TIME SUGGESTIONS

Jeremy is always boasting to Sam about his possessions. Sam's imagination is more exciting to him than any of Jeremy's possessions, but we can't all be like Sam all the time. How do we feel when someone boasts to us? Use the sentence stem below to explore this area further.

'When someone is being boastful, I feel . . .'

Each time Jeremy boasts about something, he has some kind of mishap. These experiences could be an illustration of the saying 'Pride comes before a fall.' Are you sometimes guilty of too much pride, like Jeremy? Have you shown off about something?

Sentence stem

'Something I have boasted about is . . .'

This could be a skill, a possession, a mark for some school work, or a reading level.

After the round using the sentence above, encourage children to think of ways in which they can prevent themselves from being boastful.

FOLLOW-UP ACTIVITIES

• Hidden in the illustrations of *Look What I've Got!* are some common sayings or phrases. Can you spot the walls that have ears? What kind of dog should you beware of? Think of other sayings or phrases and talk about what they mean. Then draw them literally. For example:

> *You can't teach an old dog new tricks.*
>
> *Not enough room to swing a cat.*
>
> *Eyes in the back of your head.*
>
> *Wear your heart on your sleeve.*
>
> *Don't look a gift horse in the mouth.*
>
> *Butterflies in the stomach.*
>
> *Frog in the throat.*
>
> *Skeleton in the cupboard.*
>
> *All fingers and thumbs.*

• Design some pictures with hidden objects or references within them. These could be used as part of a display called 'What Sam Saw'. You could extend the theme by exploring other books by Anthony Browne that use this idea. There are some titles listed below. We have tried to include books that are visually interesting and tie in with themes explored in this book. All these titles should be readily available from your local library or bookshop, if you don't have them in your school.

The Tunnel (Walker Books Ltd, 1997)

The Night Shimmy (Corgi Children's Books, 2003)

Gorilla (Walker Books Ltd, 1995)

The Visitors Who Came to Stay (Walker Books Ltd, 2000)

Look What I've Got!

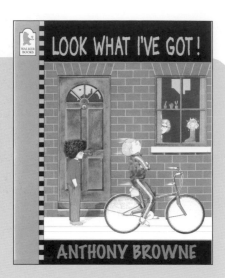

BOOK DETAILS

Author and illustrator:
Anthony Browne

Publisher: Walker Books Ltd
(1996)

ISBN: 0 7445 4372 X

TOPICS

✓ *Making the most of every day*

✓ *Understanding differences*

✓ *Using our imagination*

✓ *Valuing special things*

✓ *Jealousy*

SUMMARY OF STORY

Jeremy always has new things – a bicycle, a pirate outfit, a bag of sweets – and he always boasts about them to Sam. But Sam doesn't seem bothered or jealous, and uses his imagination to see exciting things in the world around him that make his life far from dull.

THINGS TO THINK ABOUT

This book can be seen from two perspectives: Sam's and Jeremy's. In many ways, they connect only occasionally. It is really important to read the book through once without interruption, because it is only at the end of the book that you will understand Sam's perspective.

Why has Anthony Browne chosen the title *Look What I've Got!*? It is easy to see what Jeremy has, but what does Sam have? Jeremy has lots of material possessions, but Sam is the one with the powerful imagination.

THINGS TO TALK ABOUT

- How would you feel if Jeremy said 'Look what I've got!' to you? Has someone ever said this to you? Tell me a bit more about it.

- Do Jeremy's possessions bring him much pleasure? Have you heard the saying 'Pride comes before a fall'? What do you think it means?

- Sam doesn't have possessions like Jeremy's. However, he does have a wonderful imagination, a kind heart and self-possession. Where in the book can we see each of these things?

- Sam's imagination is present on every page. Look closely at the illustrations:

    Can you spot the cow in the sitting room?

    How many people or things are frightened by the gorilla?

    Where is the chocolate bar brick?

- Look at the scene in the park with the lamp-posts. How many fish can you find?

- What are the other people in the park doing?

- Look at the scene with the washing line. Can you spot the X, Y and Z pants? Jeremy is eating a lolly, but where is the ice-cream cone? What kind of dog should you beware of? (Clue: you can eat it.)

- Find the two pages where Jeremy has his eyes wide open. What has happened to cause him to open his eyes?

- Sam sees many small details and his imagination makes them interesting or funny. Look at the last page of the book. What does he see in the woods?

THINGS TO DO OR MAKE

See if you can borrow other Anthony Browne books from school or the local library. They are full of visual jokes and messages and will be a lot of fun to share with your child. Some of his books are listed below.

The Tunnel (Walker Books Ltd, 1997); *The Night Shimmy* (Corgi Children's Books, 2003)

Gorilla (Walker Books Ltd, 1995); *The Visitors Who Came to Stay* (Walker Books Ltd, 2000)

Willy the Wimp (Walker Books Ltd, 1995); *Zoo* (Red Fox Picture Books, 1994)

The Shape Game (Corgi Children's Books, 2004); *Piggybook* (Walker Books Ltd, 1996)

Play cloudbusting. Lie on your backs and look up at the clouds. Using your imagination, what can you see? We did this one day and we saw a mountain range, a grumpy face, a harbour, a heart and an elephant. Share what you can see with each other and find out if you agree.

Spotting the beauty in every day:

Look at the last picture in the book. Sam sees unusual creatures where Jeremy would see only trees. Look at bark, leaves, tiles, cracks in the pavement and try to see pictures in the shapes they make. Perhaps you could tell stories about the things you see.

Go for a walk and try to find minibeasts (insects, bugs, creepy-crawlies), spiders' webs, birds' nests, animal tracks. Make sure you do not disturb them.

Lay a piece of string down on the ground to make a circle. Look at everything inside it.

Get a patterned piece of paper (e.g. wrapping paper or wallpaper). Cut out two pieces about A5 size. Turn one piece over and draw a favourite animal on the plain side. Cut the animal out and turn it back to the patterned side. Now stick it onto the other piece of paper, but don't line up the patterns. Your animal will be cleverly camouflaged!

Something Else

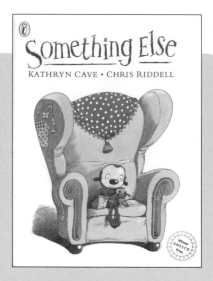

TOPICS

✓ *Friendship and belonging*

✓ *Understanding differences*

✓ *Bullying*

✓ *Inclusion*

SUMMARY OF STORY

Something Else wants to be like everyone else, but he's different and no one wants to play with him. One day an even odder creature called Something turns up at Something Else's house. Something Else is not sure he wants to be with him, but soon they find ways to be firm friends. And when something really strange in the shape of a boy appears, they make room for him too.

TALKING POINTS

• How did Something Else feel when the other creatures would not let him join in with them?

• How could the other creatures have acted differently towards Something Else?

• Do you think that the other creatures were rude or uncaring towards Something Else?

• Where do you think Something came from?

• What feelings did Something Else have towards Something?

• What caused his feelings to change?

• How do we feel about being friends with people who are different?

• Why might it be difficult to befriend unusual people?

• Why can it be hard for someone to be included in a group?

• How could you help someone join in a group?

• Should we judge people by appearance only?

• Why is it right to include others in a group? How might everyone benefit?

Author: Kathryn Cave   Illustrator: Chris Riddell
Publisher: Puffin Books (1995)   ISBN: 0 14 054907 2

CIRCLE-TIME SUGGESTIONS

Cross the Circle. This game mixes the children in the circle up nicely, changing the dynamics of the group. Use instructions such as the following to achieve this. This requires lots of honesty from the children, so make sure your circle has a sound non-judgemental ethos.

Swap places with someone in the circle if you have ever deliberately shut someone out of your group.

Swap places with someone in the circle if you have ever felt really sorry for someone who was left out.

Swap places with someone in the circle if you have ever called anyone 'sad'.

Swap places with someone in the circle if you have ever felt left out of a group.

Ask each child to turn to the person on their left and to think of something that's special about them. When it's their turn, they say: 'This is my friend . . . and they are special because . . . [say why they are special].'

Sentence stem

'Sometimes I don't let people join in because . . .'

Children will attempt to legitimise their desire not to play with unpopular children by offering excuses like 'The game is full' or 'The sides will be uneven.' If they really wanted to include someone, they would find a way round these problems. If we permit this legitimising of exclusion, we will see the formation of in-groups and out-groups and the rise of the 'popular' children in our classroom. You will need this and other circle times to confront the real reasons why certain children are excluded. In the subsequent circle times it is important to encourage children to confront their prejudices and find ways through them, leading to a more inclusive and accepting life.

FOLLOW-UP ACTIVITIES

• These activities may be better suited to small-group work. Use the feelings chart on page 109 to draw and write about how Something Else feels through the book. As you read the story, mark how Something Else's feelings fluctuate during the story. Put horizontal lines to mark these points on the thermometer. You could add labels next to these marks to indicate which part of the story they refer to. You can do the same thing with the range of faces, colouring them in and labelling them. You could adapt the sheet to look at how the other characters feel.

• There is a photocopiable sheet on page 110 that should be sent home with the 'For home' material for *Something Else*.

• Display some feeling charts on a display board and surround them with the children's ideas for how the characters in *Something Else* might have been kinder to Something Else.

• If you see some good co-operative play going on, you might take a digital photograph of the cheering incident. Put this on the display board too.

Something Else

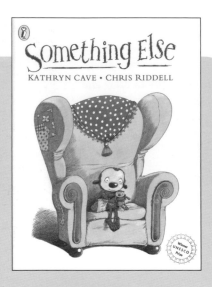

BOOK DETAILS

Author: Kathryn Cave

Illustrator: Chris Riddell

Publisher: Puffin Books (1995)

ISBN: 0 14 054907 2

TOPICS

✓ *Friendship and belonging*

✓ *Understanding differences*

✓ *Bullying*

✓ *Inclusion*

SUMMARY OF STORY

Something Else wants to be like everyone else, but he's different and no one wants to play with him. One day an even odder creature called Something turns up at Something Else's house. Something Else is not sure he wants to be with him, but soon they find ways to be firm friends. And when something really strange in the shape of a boy appears, they make room for him too.

THINGS TO THINK ABOUT

• As an adult, have you ever felt like Something Else? Have you ever felt left out of a group socially or at work?

• Have you ever made a conscious effort to include an isolated adult? What did you do?

• Did you ever bully anyone at school or did you ever feel bullied?

• What was done to help those involved in bullying to get along better with each other?

THINGS TO TALK ABOUT

• Why was Something Else sad?

• What did the creatures in the story say to him?

• How did Something Else try to be included in the group?

• What went wrong?

• Who did all the trying in the part of the story where Something Else wants to be part of the group?

• Do you sometimes feel worried about being friends with people who are a bit different?

• What are some of the difficulties and dangers around being friends with people who are a bit different?

• Who is in your group at school?

• Whose group would you like to be in?

• Why would you like to be in the group of your choice?

• When Something turned up in the story, Something Else didn't want him around at first, but then he changed his mind. See if you can see when he changed his mind.

• What did Something Else say to Something?

• Why was he kind to Something?

• Do you think he knew how Something felt?

• What sort of things did Something Else and Something do together?

- **What sorts of things do we do together in our family?**

- **What other things would you like us to do together?**

- **Do you think anyone in our family sometimes feels left out?**

- **Do we ever do things that leave people out?**

- **What can we do to include them?**

THINGS TO DO OR MAKE

What games can we all play together at home? Suppose we got a cardboard box, labelled it 'The Sharing Box' and put in it one or two toys or books we were happy to share with each other. Let's find a time to play together. When would be a good time for this?

Use the photocopiable sheet supplied with these notes to stick some pictures of your family on and round the armchair. You could put it up somewhere prominent as a reminder of who makes up your family. When you are going to do something together, you could make a label saying what the activity will be and put it next to the photocopiable sheet. Make a celebration of this event so that it builds up a sense of anticipation.

Making a new friend. Invite to your house someone whom you have not spent much time with before. Look at the activities that Something and Something Else do together. Could you do these or similar activities with your new friend? You could make some sandwiches, pack them up and go somewhere for a picnic. That might be the sitting room, your garden or any safe place.

Slow Loris

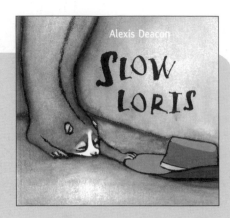

TOPICS

✓ *Friendship and belonging*

✓ *Understanding differences*

✓ *Transfer to a new school*

✓ *Exploring reputation*

SUMMARY OF STORY

Everyone thought that Slow Loris was the most boring animal in the zoo. Then the other animals discovered his secret: Slow Loris was lazy during the day because he was really wild at night. When the animals realise this, they have a wonderful party with him and then sleep through the following day. Visitors to the zoo think they are all really boring, but the animals don't care because now they have a secret too.

TALKING POINTS

• Why do you think Slow Loris didn't much care for living in the zoo?

• What activities does Slow Loris do slowly?

• Look at the visitors who come to see Slow Loris. How do they react to him?

• How do they describe him?

• How would you feel if someone described you as boring?

• How does Slow Loris feel about being thought of as boring?

• Is it always easy to ignore other people's opinions, as Slow Loris does?

• What gives Slow Loris the confidence to do so?

• What activities does Slow Loris do quickly?

• What does Slow Loris wear in the night?

• What do you think these clothes tell us about Slow Loris?

• The meerkats discover Slow Loris's secret. How do you think they feel about it?

• How do you think the other animals feel when they first hear about Slow Loris's secret?

• How does it change their opinion of him?

• What do the other animals wear in the night? What effect do you think these outfits have on their behaviour?

• Have you ever found something out that changed your opinion of someone?

• Do you have a secret side like Slow Loris?

• What would other people be surprised to learn about you?

MOTIONS FOR DEBATE

'This class believes that first impressions count.'

'This class believes that you can't judge a book by its cover.'

These are two contrasting statements to explore. Handled carefully, they can lead to some interesting reassessment of how children make judgements about each other.

Author and illustrator: Alexis Deacon
Publisher: Red Fox Picture Books (2003)   ISBN: 0 09 941426 0

CIRCLE-TIME SUGGESTIONS

Slow Loris is confident in his own abilities. He isn't worried when others think he is boring. Can we develop our own self-confidence in the same way? In honour of Slow Loris, pass a hat around the circle instead of a speaking object as you explore the sentence stems below.

Sentence stems

'Something that gives me confidence is . . .'

'My hidden talent is . . .'

FOLLOW-UP ACTIVITIES

• **If you were an animal, what animal would you be?**

   Are you like Slow Loris, quiet when people are around but wild when no one is looking?

   Are you loyal like a dog?   Are you brave like a lion?

   Are you stubborn like a donkey?   Are you as clever as a monkey?

These statements about themselves could be used as the basis of a poem. See 'The Writer of this Poem' in *Sky in the Pie* by Roger McGough (Puffin Books, 2003) as an example of a poem structure for this activity.

• **What characteristics do other animals have? This could link with work in literacy on similes. Each child could write a short poem about their family or friends being similar to different animals. For example:**

My father is like a bear, sleeping in his den.

My mother is like a bird, feathering our nest.

My brother is like a monkey, swinging from the furniture.

And I am a cat, curled up in my favourite chair.

These poems could work well with actions alongside them. Children could work in pairs to develop dramatised readings of their poems, swapping roles depending on whose poem is being read.

• **Buddies and pals. This is a system to help integrate children into a group. Once it is set up, it can be used to support children who are new to school, or children who are struggling, either with work or friendships. Ask for volunteers from your class to be buddies. Match each with a child who needs a little support, the pal. Encourage the buddy to introduce themselves to the pal and find out how to help the pal. They might be a study buddy. They might spend some break times together. The buddy might show the pal around the school or explain some school systems. The buddies could run Buddy and Pal clubs at break times, for any pals to attend. For more information about buddies and pals and how they can be used as a school-wide system, see *Stay Cool in School* by Margaret Goldthorpe, published by the Bible Reading Fellowship in 2003.**

Slow Loris

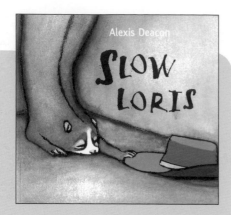

BOOK DETAILS

Author and illustrator: Alexis Deacon

Publisher: Red Fox Picture Books (2003)

ISBN: 0 09 941426 0

TOPICS

✓ *Friendship and belonging*

✓ *Understanding differences*

✓ *Transfer to a new school*

✓ *Exploring reputation*

SUMMARY OF STORY

Everyone thought that Slow Loris was the most boring animal in the zoo. Then the other animals discovered his secret: Slow Loris was lazy during the day because he was really wild at night. When the animals realise this, they have a wonderful party with him and then sleep through the following day. Visitors to the zoo think they are all really boring, but the animals don't care because now they have a secret too.

THINGS TO THINK ABOUT

• Slow Loris is an outsider at the zoo until the other animals discover that there is more to him than meets the eye. We have all been in situations where we feel like an outsider, perhaps when starting a new school or job.

• Just as people won't know the real us until they take the time to find out, sometimes we have to think that maybe we don't know everything about our neighbours and colleagues. Sometimes you have to spend time with people before you find out how truly interesting they are.

• Slow Loris has great self-confidence. He doesn't change to suit the zoo, the visitors or the other animals. He is who he is, and when the animals get to know him, they like him.

• The animals think that Slow Loris is boring, but he has another side to him. Equally, children often think that all their parents do is work and tell them off. Do you have another side that your children don't see very much? For example, do you go salsa dancing in the evenings? Or grow vegetables in an allotment, or play snooker in a local hall? Now could be a good time to share your enthusiasm with your children.

THINGS TO TALK ABOUT

• What does Slow Loris do slowly? Why does he do these things slowly?

• What do the visitors who come to see Slow Loris feel about him?

• Slow Loris doesn't really fit in at the zoo. Have you ever been somewhere you didn't fit in?

• How did it make you feel?

• What does Slow Loris do quickly? Why does he do these things quickly?

• How many different hats does Slow Loris wear?

• News of Slow Loris's secret life spreads rapidly. How do you think the other animals felt when they heard about it?

• What do they think about Slow Loris after they discover his secret?

• Do you have a secret life like Slow Loris?

• What would other people think about you if they knew about your secret life?

THINGS TO DO OR MAKE

As a family, go through some old magazines or clothes catalogues, and cut out clothes and accessories you would each like to wear if you could have a secret life like Slow Loris. Perhaps Mum will find a fabulous evening dress. Perhaps Dad would like to wear a diving suit. Maybe Grandma would like to be a pirate, a ballerina, a sumo wrestler, a film star at a premiere or a sports star. If you can't find the right outfit or accessories, draw them on the card where you are sticking the cut-out pieces. Any base board will do – the back of a cereal packet would be fine. If you have some spare family photographs, you could cut out the heads and stick them above your chosen outfits. Put this display on the fridge door for everyone to see.

You could have a special Slow Loris tea that you organise, with a few little treats. If you want to go one step further, you could each have a go at making your special Slow Loris hat from any materials you have around the house. You could wear these on special occassions.

Fold a piece of A4 paper in half. Ask your child to draw themselves in their school uniform on one half. On the other half, they should draw themselves in their Slow Loris outfit – the clothes that show the real them. Slow Loris dresses up in different hats and ties. What do they wear when they have the choice?

Transition toolbox. If your child is facing transition to a new school, put together a transition toolbox to help them with the move. Working with your child, make a booklet of useful information (a map of their route to school, the school's address and contact details, a menu of food they would like to have in their packed lunches over the term, a list of children they already know in the new school). It can be a confidence booster for your child to have a list of their qualities and talents to take to their new school. This list can be contributed to by friends, teachers from the old school and other family members. You will be able to think of other things to go in the toolbox.

The Smartest Giant in Town

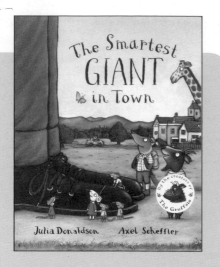

TOPICS

✓ *Helping others*
✓ *Making the most of every day*
✓ *Doing the right thing*
✓ *Making choices*
✓ *Being a hero*

SUMMARY OF STORY

George is the scruffiest giant in town, until one day he buys himself some new clothes. But on the way home he gives them away to various animals whose needs are greater than his. Eventually George goes back to the shop to buy some more clothes. Unfortunately, the shop is shut and he has to make do with his old clothes, which he finds in a bag by the shop door. The animals George helped meet him and give him the gift of a gold paper crown and the title of the kindest giant in town.

TALKING POINTS

- Is George the only giant in town?

- Look at the first two pages. What is wrong with the town? Does everyone behave well? Is everyone happy?

- What do you think the shop keepers are going to do with George's old clothes? Can you think of a creative use for them?

- Why does George say he has given his tie away? Is this the truth?

- What do you think the lady giant is thinking?

- How does George look after he has given his tie away?

- As George gives each piece of clothing away, does he get sadder and sadder or happier and happier? Why do you think that is?

- When George's trousers fall down, how does he feel?

- Why doesn't he ask for all his clothes back? Could we understand it if he had done that?

- When George returns to the clothes shop, what does he find has happened? What does he find by the side of the shop?

- How does George describe his old clothes?

- What did the animals give George?

- What did they want to show George by their gift?

- Why didn't they give George clothes to replace those he gave away? (Perhaps they didn't have the money or maybe they recognised that what made George wonderful wasn't his possessions, but his kindness. He was smart on the inside.)

Author: Julia Donaldson   Illustrator: Axel Scheffler
Publisher: Macmillan Children's Books (2002)   ISBN: 0 333 96396 2

CIRCLE-TIME SUGGESTIONS

This game is an adaptation of 'I went to market . . .'. In this version of the game each child says the following sentence stem: 'I am a giant and I am giving away . . .'. The first child has to choose something to give away that begins with the first letter of the alphabet. The recipient of the gift in the sentence also needs to begin with this letter of the alphabet. For example, 'I am a giant and I am giving away my anorak to an aardvark.' The next child to speak has to use the next letter of the alphabet; for example, 'I am a giant and I am giving away my boots to a bear' and so on.

Sentence stem

'Something I could give away is . . .'

Each child chooses a possession, their time or a kind act to give away.

FOLLOW-UP ACTIVITIES

• **Compose a tune for the song the animals wrote for George. You can get a story tape by Macmillan Audio Books that has George's song set to music on one side. Your version can be as involved as you choose, from a simple chant to an accompanied piece. Whatever level you choose, make sure it is enjoyable. You could find an audience to show the finished piece to – for example, a younger class, a group of parents or the lunchtime supervisors.**

• **What other items could you give away if you were George? Or a lady giant? Try to write some new lines for the song – for example, 'My skirt is a mat for a little brown cat. My comb is a rake for a gardening snake.' You could build this up as a class composition, or the children could work in pairs.**

ASSEMBLY IDEA

Use this book to introduce the idea of charitable giving. George gave away his clothes, even though it meant he ended up cold. You could have a week in school when everyone does something for charity.

Many charities have shoebox appeals. The children can bring in some small gifts such as toothbrush or toothpaste, pencils and pens, picture books, gloves, small balls, make-up, hair accessories and toy cars. They could also make some small gifts in school – for example, notepads, fleecy hats, puzzles, jewellery and a greetings card. These are then packed into empty shoeboxes and sent by a charity to children in need. Operation Christmas Child (www.samaritanspurse.uk.com) is one charity that runs such a scheme. For others, search the Internet.

During national events like Red Nose Day, the children can earn a red nose from the school by carrying out good deeds. We have asked children to perform at least five good deeds to earn their nose – for example, cleaning someone else's shoes, planting a flower in the school grounds, mending a library book, tidying an area of the school or making a pledge (I won't argue with my friends on Red Nose Day). The school has given to charity by paying for the noses, but the children have given their time and earned their red noses by their own efforts.

Charities such as World Vision and Oxfam have alternative gift catalogues (see www.worldvision.org.uk or www.oxfamunwrapped.com for details). We have shown such catalogues to children and told them that their good work and behaviour will earn points during a particular week. At the end of the week, each class can total up how many points they have earned and the school will convert this to money (from school funds) that can be spent on an alternative gift. For as little as £5 the children can buy a fruit tree for a poor family, who can eat the fruit and sell the surplus; £20 will buy a small flock of chickens.

The Smartest Giant in Town

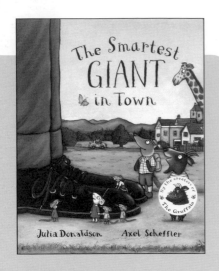

BOOK DETAILS

Author: Julia Donaldson

Illustrator: Axel Scheffler

Publisher: Macmillan

Children's Books (2002)

ISBN: 0 333 96396 2

TOPICS

✓ *Helping others*

✓ *Making the most of every day*

✓ *Doing the right thing*

✓ *Making choices*

✓ *Being a hero*

SUMMARY OF STORY

George is the scruffiest giant in town, until one day he buys himself some new clothes. But on the way home he gives them away to various animals whose needs are greater than his. Eventually George goes back to the shop to buy some more clothes. Unfortunately, the shop is shut and he has to make do with his old clothes, which he finds in a bag by the shop door. The animals George helped meet him and give him the gift of a gold paper crown and the title of the kindest giant in town.

THINGS TO THINK ABOUT

- George doesn't have very much, but what he does have he gives away to people whom he recognises as needy. This book is a good starting point for thinking about how you might as a family help others.

THINGS TO TALK ABOUT

- Look at the first two pages. What are the other giants that you can see in the town like?

- How do you think the town's inhabitants are feeling?

- What do you think the shop keepers think about George, from their expressions?

- Why did George give his tie away?

- How do George's feelings change as he gives each piece of clothing away?

- When George's trousers fall down and he is cold, does he ask everyone to give him back his gifts? Why doesn't he do that?

- Have you ever wanted to ask for a gift back?

- All the animals say 'Thank you' to George after he has helped them. Have you ever forgotten to say thank you and felt sorry afterwards?

- What did the animals give George?

- What were they saying thank you for?

- Why didn't they give him clothes? (Perhaps they didn't have the money, or maybe they recognised that it wasn't George's possessions that made him wonderful, but his kindness. He was smart on the inside.)

- There are lots of nursery rhyme and fairy-tale characters in the pictures. Go through the book again and see how many you can spot. Do you know which rhymes or fairy tales they are from? Can you find the princess and her frog? The three bears? One of the three little pigs? Baa, baa, black sheep? Puss in boots?

THINGS TO DO OR MAKE

Many charities have shoebox appeals. One such charity is Operation Christmas Child. Their details are as follows.

Website: www.samaritanspurse.uk.com

Address: Samaritans Purse Ltd, Victoria Road, Buckhurst Hill, Essex, IG9 5EX

Telephone: 020 8559 2044

As a family, you could fill a shoebox with some small gifts – for example, toothbrush and toothpaste, pencils and pens, picture books, gloves, small balls, make-up, hair accessories and toy cars. You could also make some small gifts, such as a notepad, a puzzle, a knitted scarf, jewellery and a greetings card. You could then send the filled shoebox to a charity that will distribute it to children in need. For other charities, search the Internet.

Blue Peter regularly has charity appeals. Watch the programme together or look on their website at www.bbc.co.uk/cbbc/bluepeter for information on their current appeal.

We all have things in our houses that we could live without – old toys, old clothes, books we don't want to re-read, unwanted Christmas presents, Play Station® games we have finished with, videos or DVDs that have been watched time and time again. As a family, have a clear out. See if each of you can contribute at least three things. Then either donate them to a charity shop or sell them at a car boot sale and give the money to a charity.

You might like to adopt one charity as a family charity to support during the course of a year.

Katie Morag Delivers the Mail

TOPICS

✓ *Responsibility and blame*

✓ *Doing the right thing*

✓ *Being honest*

✓ *Sorting out problems*

✓ *Making choices*

✓ *Forgiveness*

✓ *Asking for help*

SUMMARY OF STORY

When Katie Morag is asked to deliver the mail, she falls in a pool of water and all of the parcel labels smudge. Then she gets in a panic and does a silly thing. Katie Morag doesn't know what to do, so she just gives out the parcels to the first houses she comes to. Fortunately, when she gets to Grannie's house she tells her everything and together they sort out the muddle.

TALKING POINTS

- How are the different people in the post office feeling at the start of the story?

- What was the silly thing that Katie Morag did? Was it falling in the pool or was it not sorting out the problem with the labels straightaway?

- How did Katie Morag feel when she saw all of the parcel labels smudged so she couldn't read them?

- How do you react when you feel like that?

- How does Katie Morag decide to sort things out?

- Would you have done the same?

- What is the difference between an accident and deliberately doing something wrong?

- Have you ever had an accident, like Katie Morag, and tried to cover it up?

- Why do we worry about telling people we have made a mistake?

- What are we worried will happen?

- Sometimes people are not kind and understanding when we have done something accidentally wrong. They shout at us and tell us off. Is there anything at all we can do about that – at the time or afterwards?

- What did Katie Morag's grannie say when she heard what had happened? How did she respond to Katie Morag?

- Look at Grannie's face in the picture. What did she suggest they do next?

- How should we behave if someone accidentally upsets us or admits to a mistake?

- In what ways was Grannie helpful to Katie Morag?

- How would remembering how Katie Morag's grannie behaved help you to behave towards each other?

- Remember that Katie Morag chose to be honest and ask for help. Grannie chose not to be cross but instead to help sort out the problem.

- We cannot choose not to have accidents, but we can choose how to handle the consequences.

Author and Illustrator: Mairi Hedderwick
Publisher: Red Fox Picture Books (1984)   ISBN: 0 09 922072 5

MOTION FOR DEBATE

'This class believes that Katie Morag should have been punished for her actions.'

Katie Morag makes two mistakes in the book. First, she drops the mailbag while paddling, and then she panics and delivers the parcels haphazardly. Should she have been punished for both or either of these mistakes?

FOLLOW-UP ACTIVITIES

• Go through the book with the class. Look at the expression on Katie Morag's face at each stage of the story. Discuss how it changes. What is the moment when things improve?

• Make a timeline of the story on a strip of paper, labelling each of the main events in the story. Draw Katie Morag's face in the top left-hand corner of the timeline. Above the line write several words that illustrate how she is feeling at each stage of the story. Record Grannie's face alongside Katie Morag's feelings as she appears in the story.

• There is a photocopiable sheet on page 108 that should be sent home with the 'For home' material for *Katie Morag Delivers the Mail*.

ASSEMBLY IDEA

Ask each class to read *Katie Morag Delivers the Mail* during the week preceding the assembly. All staff will need briefing about the assembly as some of them will have very small speaking parts. Ask a (prepared and game) colleague to open the assembly for you. They should not mention the book. They should call you out and give you a large bundle of 'very important letters for the teachers' with the instruction 'Don't get these muddled up.' These will be junk mail, collected previously. Having given their complicated and detailed instructions about whom all the letters should be delivered to, they should heap the bundle up in your arms and leave the assembly hall. You immediately become very agitated about the job and in your agitation drop the pile. You then decide you have to carry out the task and arbitrarily hand the letters out to the staff. They can then complain loudly that they have the wrong post – for example, 'Why have you given me the Year 6 SATs papers? I teach Year 4!', 'I'm not interested in a football catalogue. I'm the music teacher! Where is my *Tuba Monthly*?' You turn to the children and ask for help. What do they think you should have done at each stage? What could you have done when you were first given the mail? What should you have done when you dropped it?

Get real, get right, get going. See the activity on page 91. Use the poster on page 108 to talk about ways to sort out problems in school.

Katie Morag Delivers the Mail

BOOK DETAILS

Author and Illustrator: Mairi Hedderwick

Publisher: Red Fox Picture Books (1984)

ISBN: 0 09 922072 5

TOPICS

✓ *Responsibility and blame*

✓ *Doing the right thing*

✓ *Being honest*

✓ *Sorting out problems*

✓ *Making choices*

✓ *Forgiveness*

✓ *Asking for help*

SUMMARY OF STORY

When Katie Morag is asked to deliver the mail, she falls in a pool of water and all of the parcel labels smudge. Then she gets in a panic and does a silly thing. Katie Morag doesn't know what to do, so she just gives out the parcels to the first houses she comes to. Fortunately, when she gets to Grannie's house she tells her everything and together they sort out the muddle.

THINGS TO THINK ABOUT

What was the problem with Katie Morag's behaviour? It wasn't the fact that she went paddling, that's normal. It wasn't dropping the bag, that was just an accident. It wasn't crying, that was an understandable reaction. The problem with Katie Morag's behaviour was that she tried to cover up her mistake (and naturally the people who got the wrong parcels were cross). What she should have done was be honest and immediately seek help. Mistakes happen. It is our response to mistakes that makes the difference. Grannie taught Katie Morag how to make a good response. Grannie handled the situation well. She didn't lose her temper, she simply got on and showed Katie Morag how to put things right. She was a good role model.

THINGS TO TALK ABOUT

- Katie Morag is a good, helpful girl. What were the problems in the post office that morning? (Look at the first double-page spread for clues.)

- How did she help to make things at home better?

- When Katie Morag was asked to help, did she complain? Have a look at her face in the picture.

- Paddling looked fun. Was the paddling a problem for Katie Morag?

- What might she have done with the bag of parcels to avoid any mishap while she was paddling?

- How did Katie Morag feel when she realised what had happened to the parcels?

- What did she do with the wet parcels?

- What was the problem with what she decided to do?

- What could she have done differently?

- Grannie was brilliant at helping to sort things out.

- Look at her face and what she says when Katie Morag is drying off. How is Grannie feeling?

- What other problems can you see Grannie has sorted out? (Look at Katie Morag's wet clothes. Look at the chicks.)

- What is in Grannie's hand and what is it for?

- What problems had Katie Morag created by her actions?

- How did she and Grannie sort them out?

- Which part of the story is about an accident and which is about being silly?

- How much worse would the problem have been if Katie Morag had not been honest and told her grannie everything?

THINGS TO DO OR MAKE

Think about the last time someone did a silly thing at home and there was a row as a result. How could you sort the same kind of problem out better next time? Below is a way you could try.

Katie Morag learned that she had to:

Face up to things – Get real.

Choose to get help from someone sensible and kind – Get right.

Sort things out – Get going!

Remember: *Get real*   *Get right*   *Get going!*

Use the poster supplied with these notes next time there is a problem at home so you can plan a way to solve it peacefully. Remember – most things can be sorted out without getting cross.

Sending postcards. Buy some plain postcards. Decorate them however you like. You might draw pictures, make a tiny collage or stick on a photograph. Send them to your relatives, with two or three sentences about something enjoyable you have done recently. Write RSVP on them, and wait for a reply.

Packages. Get a piece of A4 paper. Imagine it is a parcel you will be receiving. Look through a magazine and cut out pictures of things you would like to find in your parcel. Stick them onto the paper. Address it to yourself on the back and put some ribbon and string around it.

Amazing Grace

Mary Hoffman · Caroline Binch

TOPICS

✓ *Worries and fears*

✓ *Understanding differences*

✓ *Making choices*

SUMMARY OF STORY

Grace wants to be Peter Pan in the school play. However, even though she knows she would be brilliant, some unkind children tell her she can't do this because she is a girl and black. They try to make Grace doubt herself and shake her confidence. But Grace's wise nana helps her to keep her confidence in her abilities.

TALKING POINTS

- Grace lives for stories – she likes to tell them and act them out. From whom does she get this talent?

- Look at Grace's face when she is being told a story. How does this help to tell you how she is feeling?

- Does Grace act out her stories on her own? Who and what else does she involve in her plays?

- When Grace acts out a story, who appears to be in charge?

- Is Grace a leader or a follower in these situations?

- What kind of parts does she take in her plays?

- Why do you think the other children follow Grace and let her be the leader?

- Look at the props and costumes Grace uses for her plays. Are they all bought from shops? Look at her when she is Anansi. What has she made the spider's legs from?

- Do you think Grace's family is rich? Do you think you need to be rich to put on exciting plays at home or in your classroom?

- Two children tell Grace she can't be Peter Pan because she is black and a girl. Why do you think they say this? Was it a kind thing to say? Was it a true thing to say?

- Why was it wrong of Raj and Natalie to say the things they did?

- How do their comments make Grace feel? Look at her face when she tells her family about their comments.

- Why do you think that Grace's mum starts to get angry?

- Would it have helped if Grace had got angry with Raj and Natalie at school?

- Does getting angry usually fail as a method of achieving justice?

- Nana has a better idea for helping Grace. She decides to take her to see someone who is hugely successful and comes from a family just like Grace's. What does Nana want Grace to learn from seeing Rosalie Wilkins dance?

- What does Grace say to herself when she is playing being a ballet dancer?

- How has Nana helped Grace to get the part of Peter Pan?

- What might have happened if Nana had not taken her to see Rosalie Wilkins? Imagine some of the alternative outcomes to the story.

Author: Mary Hoffman   Illustrator: Caroline Binch
Publisher: Frances Lincoln Ltd (1991)   ISBN: 0 7112 0699 6

- Is it true that Grace could be anything she wanted to be?

- Grace did get to be Peter Pan. What about the other children who also wanted to be Peter Pan – could they be anything that they wanted to be?

- Sometimes, despite our best efforts, we don't get to be what we want to be. If Grace had been disappointed, how might her family have helped?

MOTION FOR DEBATE

'This class believes that if you put your mind to it, you can do anything you want to do.'

People often say that if you put your mind to it you can do anything. Certainly people sometimes do amazing things. It is important to encourage these characteristics in children. However, is it more realistic to recognise our limitations alongside our strengths?

FOLLOW-UP ACTIVITIES

- Make a big display of all of the ideas about methods of encouragement raised in the circle time. Include examples of school methods of encouragement.

- You may want to discuss how we handle situations when people mock, decry or denigrate us. What sort of things should we say or do? Role-play some scenarios. You could focus on developing polite ways of asking people to stop, ways of speaking positively to yourselves and finding an adult to assist. You could also role-play poor reactions to such taunting and how these make the situation worse. You could freeze the role play just before it escalates into conflict, and explore more positive ways in which the taunted child could have reacted.

CIRCLE-TIME SUGGESTIONS

Have a circle time that explores skills and abilities. Go round the circle, allowing each child to complete the sentence stem:

'The thing I like best / enjoy most / am best at is . . .'

You could have a second circle time to discuss ways in which we can encourage each other. If you introduce this idea a couple of days before the circle time, you can ask the children to talk to their families and get them to think of times and ways they have been encouraged to achieve things. You can also think of incentives that encourage the children at school (stickers, show and tell, merit marks, certificates and so on).

The children can share what they found out from home or complete this sentence stem:

'I felt encouraged when . . .'

Amazing Grace

BOOK DETAILS

Author: Mary Hoffman

Illustrator: Caroline Binch

Publisher: Frances Lincoln Ltd (1991)

ISBN: 0 7112 0699 6

TOPICS

✓ *Worries and fears*

✓ *Understanding differences*

✓ *Making choices*

SUMMARY OF STORY

Grace wants to be Peter Pan in the school play. However, even though she knows she would be brilliant, some unkind children tell her she can't do this because she is a girl and black. They try to make Grace doubt herself and shake her confidence. But Grace's wise nana helps her to keep her confidence in her abilities.

THINGS TO THINK ABOUT

It is very important that we know the things our children are good at, and encourage and develop these skills and talents. Grace's family recognise her acting and storytelling skills and know that it would be wrong for her to believe the children who tried to discourage her. Being a girl or being black plainly should never be allowed to stop Grace from doing what she is good at.

Sometimes the skills and talents our children have are not the ones we want them to have. This can lead us into having hopeless ambitions for our children – for example, wanting them to be good at sports or musical when in fact they are artistic or knowledgeable about the natural world. This is why it is important that we give our children every opportunity to discover what they like and can do well, and then help them to shine at those things. This might mean putting our dreams aside so that they can pursue theirs.

Play is very important for children because it helps them to understand the world and enjoy being part of it. Television is a passive activity and it is not a good idea for it to occupy a lot of a child's time. This means that you may have to be proactive in encouraging them to do other things. Once children have good play habits they are more likely to read, play with their toys, play make-believe games, act out stories by themselves and with their brothers and sisters and so on. You may have to encourage them by playing with them at first.

Rosalie is a wonderful role model for Grace. Talk about what makes a good role model. Who might be a good one for your child, your family or even for you?

THINGS TO TALK ABOUT

- **From whom do you think Grace has inherited her skills at telling stories? What makes you think that?**

- **Do you think Grace is a leader or a follower? How can you tell?**

- **Who are her friends? Are they all human or even alive?**

- **In what ways are Mum and Nana good at playing with Grace?**

- **What do they do to help her play?**

- **Look at the dressing-up clothes and the props Grace has when she is playing. Who do you think helps her to find and make these things?**

- **Think about Nana's way of encouraging Grace. Why does Nana take Grace to the ballet?**

- **Why does she want Grace to see the photographs outside first?**

- **What sort of person do you think Rosalie's grandmother is?**

- **In what way is she like Grace's nana?**

- **Do you think Rosalie's grandmother encouraged her?**

- Why does seeing Rosalie dance encourage Grace?

- Why does it make her say, 'I can be anything I want. I can even be Peter Pan'?

- Why did the entire class vote for Grace to be Peter Pan?

- Why did Grace feel as if she could fly home at the end of the evening?

- Have you ever felt as Grace does at the end of the story?

THINGS TO DO OR MAKE

Have you ever been told that you can't do something and then been so encouraged by someone who believed in you that you have gone on to be successful? If so, talk to your child about this event.

Discuss with your child the talents and skills that they have and think of something you can do to encourage these at home. Be very specific: for example, 'You are very good at painting pictures. Why don't we get a little paint box from the supermarket so you can paint a birthday card for Nan? She would like one painted by you much more than any we could buy.'

How many of the stories that Grace acts out do you know? Can you find some in the local library and read them with your children?

Can you act out scenes from some of these stories with your children? Not all children like acting out stories, but most do. You might find that they need you to take a lead at first. If you really hate acting, you can still join in with the game. Have a look at the page where Grace's mum and grandmother are patients for Dr Grace.

Getting a dressing-up box together is fun. None of the content needs to be bought ready made from shops. A collection of old scarves, hats and belts is a good start. Save unusual clothes, shoes, boots and hats that have gone out of fashion. You can keep an eye out in charity shops for useful cheap items. Some of these can be good birthday or Christmas presents. We know one parent who spent time looking for three old bridesmaid dresses in charity shops. They also collected a pirate outfit consisting of a stripy T-shirt, shorts, socks, a cheap plastic cutlass and an eye patch from a chemist. They washed and mended, and wrapped everything in tissue paper. On Christmas morning their three daughters and son were thrilled with their dressing-up clothes. This was the start of a dressing-up collection. Over the next ten years the children were princes and princesses, kings and queens, knights, cowboys, Native Americans, aliens and Victorians; and acted out stories from books, films and even school history lessons. The bridesmaid dresses were worn until they were knee length on the girls and had long since ceased to do up at the back.

Discuss how we could handle disappointment. Sometimes we do not get the part in the play, the solo in the concert or the place in the team. How do we handle that? Talk about losing gracefully as well as thinking about other skills and talents that we have that we can pursue instead.

Dogger

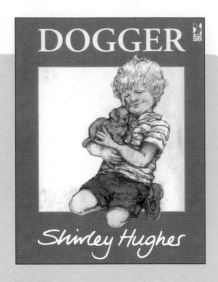

TOPICS

✓ *Worries and fears*

✓ *Living with siblings*

✓ *Helping others*

✓ *Doing the right thing*

✓ *Being part of a family*

✓ *Sorting out problems*

✓ *Valuing special things*

✓ *Being a hero*

✓ *Asking for help*

SUMMARY OF STORY

When Dave loses his favourite toy, Dogger, he is desolate. But when Dogger turns up at the school summer fair, everything seems all right – until someone buys him before Dave can get the money. Bella, Dave's sister, is able to get Dogger back by trading him for a big yellow teddy bear that she won in a raffle. Dave slept much better that night.

TALKING POINTS

• Why do you think Dogger was so special to Dave?

• What are the things that are special to you?

• What makes them special?

• Who else had special things in the book?

• Why do you think they were special to them?

• How should we treat other people's special things?

• What did each member of Dave's family do to help him find Dogger when Dave realised he had lost him? (Talk about how much time his mum and dad gave up.)

• How did Dave feel when Dogger couldn't be found? (Talk about a time when you lost something, how you felt and what the outcome was.)

• Do you remember a time when you felt like Dave?

• Look at the double-page spread of the summer fair. What is happening at the fair?

• How do you think Dave felt when Bella won the teddy bear?

• Have you ever found it difficult to be happy for someone when you are feeling sad?

• From the moment that Dave sees Dogger on the toy stall, he experiences a rollercoaster of emotions. (You could draw this as a wave, adding labels to show which each rise and fall signifies in the story.) Talk about what emotions he feels throughout the rest of the story.

• What did the little girl do that was unkind?

• What could she have done differently?

• What did Bella do that was kind to Dave?

• What might someone who was not as kind as Bella have done instead?

• That night, what did Bella say that was kind? Why was it a kind thing to say?

MOTION FOR DEBATE

'This class believes that the little girl at the summer fair should have just given Dogger back to Dave.'

The little girl returned Dogger to Dave only once she was offered something in return – Bella's new teddy bear. Should she have just returned Dogger out of kindness?

Author and illustrator: Shirley Hughes
Publisher: Red Fox Picture Books (1993)   ISBN: 0 09 992790 X

CIRCLE-TIME SUGGESTIONS

Ask children to bring in something that is very special to them (nothing expensive or with plugs or batteries). Use the sentence stem below to explore why what each child brought in is special to them.

'This is my . . . and it is special because . . .'

This is a good circle time to explore perceived value against personal value and to reflect on how certain items that do not look like treasures can be much treasured by their owners.

FOLLOW-UP ACTIVITIES

• **You might like to display the children's special things in a corner of the classroom. Dress the corner up to show how you value these things. Agree some rules about going near the special things. The children could write postcard-sized notes about their object to add to the display.**

• **Both Bella and the little girl faced dilemmas. Pose some dilemmas your class may meet, or ask them to suggest dilemmas they have faced. You may like to discuss or role-play these to find effective solutions or ways forward. Focus on scenarios that require an act of kindness at a cost to an individual. For example:**

You are at the school fair and want to buy two badges for 10p each. Your friend would like one too but doesn't have any money. You only have 20p left. What do you do?

Your brother/sister has just dropped their apple in the dirt at playtime. You have a banana, which you love, for your snack. When they find you, do you offer to share your snack with them?

You forgot to invite someone to your birthday party and know they will be upset. However, your mum/dad has already bought all the right amount of things and will be cross if they have to get some more. Do you let your friend be upset or talk to your mum/dad?

Dogger

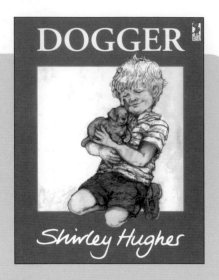

BOOK DETAILS

Author and illustrator: Shirley Hughes

Publisher: Red Fox Picture Books (1993)

ISBN: 0 09 992790 X

TOPICS

✓ *Worries and fears*

✓ *Living with siblings*

✓ *Helping others*

✓ *Doing the right thing*

✓ *Being part of a family*

✓ *Sorting out problems*

✓ *Valuing special things*

✓ *Being a hero*

✓ *Asking for help*

SUMMARY OF STORY

When Dave loses his favourite toy, Dogger, he is desolate. But when Dogger turns up at the school summer fair, everything seems all right – until someone buys him before Dave can get the money. Bella, Dave's sister, is able to get Dogger back by trading him for a big yellow teddy bear that she won in a raffle. Dave slept much better that night.

THINGS TO THINK ABOUT

We think that the reason that this book is so deeply satisfying is that it is filled with people showing love to each other. Not only do we have Bella's great act of loving sacrifice at the end of the story, but all through the story there are examples of family love too.

THINGS TO TALK ABOUT

• At the beginning of the book, how does Dave show his love for Dogger?

• Look at the page where Dave washes Dogger and the scenes outside the school gate. Talk about how the family spends time together.

• When Dogger is lost, how do Dave's mum and dad show their love for Dave? What did each member of Dave's family do to help him find Dogger? Talk about how much time his mum and dad gave up to do this.

• Spend some time looking at the summer fair. Is it like fairs at your school?

> *Can you find the child dressed as a duck?*
>
> *How much does it cost to have a lucky dip?*
>
> *Find the little boy who is trying on a jacket. How long will it take for him to grow into it?*
>
> *Who is looking at the teddy that is to be raffled?*
>
> *Can you find Dave and his family?*
>
> *Does Dave look happy?*

• Talk about Dave's feelings, from the moment when he finds Dogger until the moment when the little girl gives him up.

• Talk with your child about the last time they felt as upset as Dave. What sort of thing makes us feel that upset?

• Have a look at Bella's face when she wins the big teddy. How do you think she feels?

• Now look at Bella's face as she talks to the little girl. In particular, look at her face as she hands over the big teddy. Was this an easy decision for her to make?

• When Dogger is found and then lost again, we see that whilst Bella does love soft toys, she loves Dave more. She is selfless when she persuades the little girl to part with Dogger in exchange for the big teddy. She shows much kindness later when she tells Dave she didn't really like the teddy as he had staring eyes. It is kind and loving of her not to make Dave feel bad about her sacrifice.

• You might like to have a discussion about how brothers, sisters and other family members can show their love for each other.

THINGS TO DO OR MAKE

Collect together things that are special to all the members of your family, including children, parents and grandparents (remembering to ask them first). Talk about why they are special and about any history they may have attached to them.

If you have a camera, you might like to take photographs of all the special things and make a scrapbook. You could decorate the cover and get the people who own the special things to write something about why their item is special to them.

In the story, Dave does his washing while his mum does hers. See if you and your child can find some activities to do together at home (e.g. laundry, gardening, sewing, cooking). There are lots of overpriced sets of children's gardening and cooking utensils available, but these are not necessary. The most important part is not the equipment, but the companionship.

PHOTOCOPIABLE RESOURCES

Sharing books at home

We have been having a wonderful time sharing this story at school. We have enjoyed the story and learned a lot about our lives through it. We thought that you might like to share in this enjoyment by looking at the story with your child. Along with this story you will find material explaining how you and your child can get the most out of this particular book. The materials are designed to develop discussion between you and your child about attitudes, dilemmas, feelings and relationships, with all their ups and downs. Do ask if you have any queries. We hope you enjoy the time you spend together.

GENERAL GUIDANCE

The most effective way to approach sharing a storybook is as follows.

Prior to sharing the book with your child

- **Read the story all the way through to yourself so that you get an idea of how you might read it together.**

- **Look carefully at the illustrations. Take your time over this as they will reveal lots of details that will be of use in the discussion.**

- **Read the story out loud privately to get an idea of how to share it with your child. You can try all sorts of voices and accents if you have planned it first. This can be great fun, so be brave.**

- **Read the 'For home' material sent with this book. This will help you to know what you will be talking about and anything you might need to plan for in the 'Things to do or make' section.**

- **Annotate or highlight the 'For home' text until you feel you are ready to use it with your child. Make notes or pick out any particular questions to remind you when you are sharing the book with your child.**

With your child

- **Read the story to your child, without interruption or rushing. Choose a suitable time of the day.**

- **Re-read the story, bringing up the talking points from the 'For home' material in the way you choose as you go along.**

Each home page contains the following:

- **book details and a summary of the story;**

- **talking points to stimulate discussion with your child about the issues raised by the story and how your child might best handle the same situation;**

- **do and make ideas for you to share with your child and/or the rest of your family; these should help to reinforce the theme of the book.**

Some 'For home' pages have a 'Things to think about' section. These sections raise areas that you may need to think over before you are in a position to share them with your child.

The do and make activities are designed to be enjoyable and are not to be seen as homework. They are a chance for you to have some fun with your child and, at the same time, do some enjoyable and worthwhile activities together. You can do all or some of the activities for each book over a couple of weeks or keep them for a holiday. We might want the book back before then, but I'm sure we can come to an arrangement should you want to borrow it again for a holiday or at a later time when you are not so busy.

If you have your own ideas for activities, go ahead. Let us know how they went; we always like to have ideas for new activities.

We hope you enjoy the time that you spend with your child and the story. We hope that you both benefit from it and the things that you do together.

Classroom planning sheet

Book:

Author: *Summary of story*

Illustrator:

Publisher:

Topics

Talking points

Motion for debate

Circle-time suggestions (including games and sentence stems)

Follow-up activities

Assembly idea

Permission to Photocopy

Home planning sheet

Book:

Author:

Illustrator:

Publisher:

Topics

Things to think about

Things to talk about

Things to do or make

   Permission to Photocopy

Treasure

Morning School

I'm peeping through my window,
Waving Mum goodbye.
I feel so very sad it hurts.
I can't help it if I cry.

Mum's turning round and waving,
She's smiling at me too,
Blowing lots of kisses,
Saying 'See you soon!'

I can't help it that I cry so hard
When it's time for school to start.
I can't bear to see her walk away,
It really breaks my heart.

My teacher comes and picks me up
And dries my wet face,
Saying 'Let's get the Play-Doh out.
Come on, let's have a race!'

Soon we're making models,
Me and my friend Sue,
We're mucking about with paper
And paint, and sticky glue.

When at last it's home time
And Mummy's face appears
I'm laughing with my teacher,
I've forgotten all my tears.

From *Poems for Circle Time and the Literacy Hour* by Margaret Goldthorpe (LDA, 1998)

    Permission to Photocopy

Owl Babies

Sorting out problems

How do we sort out problems **?**

Get Real
We face up to things.

Get Right
We choose to get help from someone sensible and kind.

We don't cover up or fib.

We think about our rules.

Get Going!
We sort things out.

That's what we choose to do **!**

Feelings chart

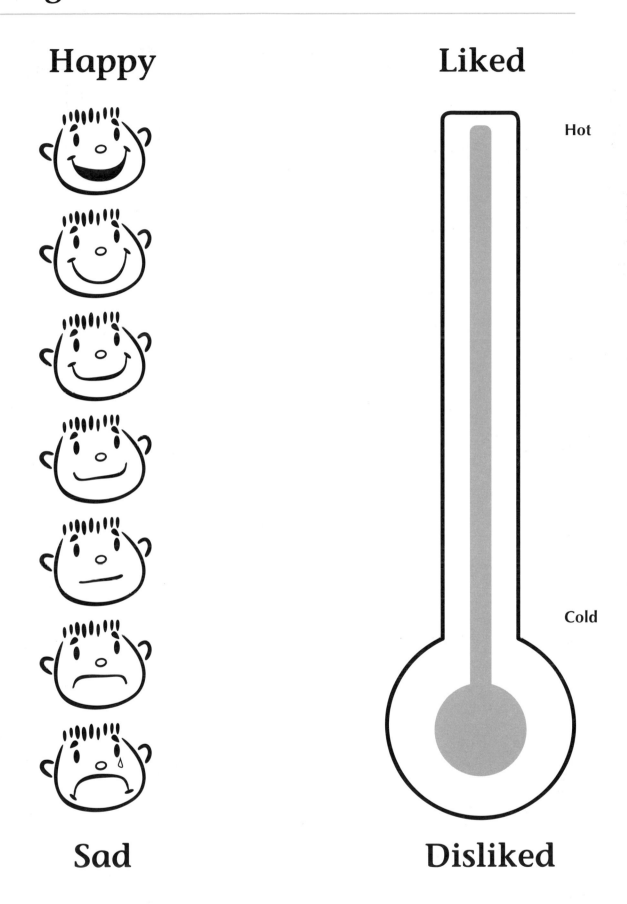

Happy

Liked

Hot

Cold

Sad

Disliked

Where does Something Else fit into the feelings chart when we first meet him?

What happened to move Something Else up the scale?

Permission to Photocopy

All together now!

 Permission to Photocopy

Training

Margaret Goldthorpe runs an INSET training company called Stay Cool in School.

If you would like further information about training for your school on any of the following topics:

- **circle time;**
- **a whole-school approach to encouraging self-discipline;**
- **dealing with difficult people;**
- **teaching RE through circle time;**
- **livelier assemblies;**

please contact:

Margaret Goldthorpe

Stay Cool in School

Midsummer Cottage

Moor Lane

Sarratt

Hertfordshire

WD3 6BY

01923 262586

dgoldthorpe@onetel.net.uk

PERMISSIONS IN ORDER OF APPEARANCE OF COVER IMAGES

All Join In © 1992 Quentin Blake (0 09 996470 8). Published by Red Fox Picture Books. Reproduced by kind permission of The Random House Group Ltd.

Mister Magnolia © 1999 Quentin Blake (0 09 940042 1). Published by Red Fox Picture Books. Reproduced by kind permission of The Random House Group Ltd.

Alfie Weather © 2002 Shirley Hughes (0 09 940425 7). Published by Red Fox Picture Books. Reproduced by kind permission of The Random House Group Ltd.

Grandfather's Pencil and the Room of Stories © 1995 Michael Foreman (0 09 950331 X). Published by Red Fox Picture Books. Reproduced by kind permission of The Random House Group Ltd.

Down the Dragon's Tongue Text © 2001 Margaret Mahy. Illustrations © Patricia MacCarthy (0 7112 1617 7). Reproduced by kind permission of the publisher, Frances Lincoln Ltd.

Owl Babies Text © 1994 Martin Waddell. Illustrations © Patrick Benson (0 7445 3167 5). Reproduced by kind permission of the publisher, Walker Books Ltd.

The Bear under the Stairs © 1994 Helen Cooper (0 552 52706 8). Published by Corgi Children's Books. Reproduced by kind permission of The Random House Group Ltd.

Lovely Old Roly Text © 2002 Michael Rosen. Illustrations © Priscilla Lamont (0 7112 1489 1). Reproduced by kind permission of the publisher, Frances Lincoln Ltd.

Oscar Got the Blame © 1995 Tony Ross (0 09 957280 X). Published by Red Fox Picture Books. Reproduced by kind permission of The Random House Group Ltd.

On the Way Home © 1982 Jill Murphy (0 333 37572 6). Reproduced by kind permission of the publisher, Macmillan Children's Books.

The True Story of the 3 Little Pigs! Text © 1991 Jon Scieszka. Illustrations © Lane Smith (0 14 054056 3). Published by Puffin Books. Reproduced by kind permission of Penguin Books Ltd.

The Princess Knight Text © 2001 Cornelia Funke. Illustrations © Kerstin Meyer (1 904442 14 5). Reproduced by kind permission of the publisher, The Chicken House.

Where the Wild Things Are © 1963 Maurice Sendak (0 09 940839 2). Published by Red Fox Picture Books. Reproduced by kind permission of The Random House Group Ltd.

Susan Laughs Text © 2001 Jeanne Willis. Illustrations © Tony Ross (0 09 940756 6). Published by Red Fox Picture Books. Reproduced by kind permission of The Random House Group Ltd.

Look What I've Got! © 1996 Anthony Browne (0 7445 4372 X). Reproduced by kind permission of the publisher, Walker Books Ltd.

Something Else Text © 1995 Kathryn Cave. Illustrations © Chris Riddell (0 14 054907 2). Published by Puffin Books. Reproduced by kind permission of Penguin Books Ltd.

Slow Loris © 2003 Alexis Deacon (0 09 941426 0). Published by Red Fox Picture Books. Reproduced by kind permission of The Random House Group Ltd.

The Smartest Giant in Town Text © 2002 Julia Donaldson. Illustrations © Axel Scheffler (0 333 96396 2). Reproduced by kind permission of the publisher, Macmillan Children's Books.

Katie Morag Delivers the Mail © 1984 Mairi Hedderwick (0 09 922072 5). Published by Red Fox Picture Books. Reproduced by kind permission of The Random House Group Ltd.

Amazing Grace Text © 1991 Mary Hoffman. Illustrations © Caroline Binch (0 7112 0699 6). Reproduced by kind permission of the publisher, Frances Lincoln Ltd.

Dogger © 1993 Shirley Hughes (0 09 992790 X). Published by Red Fox Picture Books. Reproduced by kind permission of The Random House Group Ltd.